PRESS GANGS AN

Edited by
Tony Barrow

The Bewick Press
1993

ISBN 0-9516056-9-0

© 1993 Tony Barrow

First published in Great Britain by
Bewick Press
132 Claremont Road
Whitley Bay
Tyne and Wear
NE26 3TX

with financial support from the
Historical Association

ISBN 0-9516056-9-0

Dedicated to the memory
of
JOHN PATRICK MIDDLETON
Master Mariner
(1931-1992)

CONTENTS

Foreword

It gives me great pleasure to introduce this collection of essays produced by the Newcastle upon Tyne branch of the Historical Association with a grant from the Association Development Fund, and the Bewick Press.

The Historical Association was founded nationally in 1906 to promote the study of history at all levels. A branch has met in Newcastle since 1908, with the exception of the years of the Second World War. When the branch was founded in 1908 with W.H. Hadow as its first President Newcastle looked very much to the sea and sailing ships were still a common sight on the river Tyne. It is therefore fitting in 1993, when the Quayside and river will burst into life briefly with the visit of the Tall Ships, that this collection of essays concerned with Privateering and the Press Gang should be produced in association with the Bewick Press.

The Bewick Press came into being in 1990. It was started by two former lecturers at Newcastle upon Tyne Polytechnic, Ray Challinor and Archie Potts, to fill the gap left by the retirement from publishing of Frank Graham who published 373 local history titles between 1958 and 1987 selling three million copies. From its office in Whitley Bay the Bewick Press provides a publishing outlet for local historians to market their works. It is a non profit making operation and any profits are ploughed back to keep down the cost of publication of new titles. This volume is the ninth title to be published.

The branch is indebted to Dr. N.A.M. Rodger, Dr. David J. Starkey and to Professor Norman McCord for allowing their work to be republished, and to Dr. Tony Barrow for contributing his essays. Without Tony's persistent enthusiasm this collection of essays would never have been published.

Peter Kenyon
Branch President
April 1993

LIST OF ILLUSTRATIONS

INTRODUCTION

Generations of merchant seamen have found employment on ships that sailed to every part of the world from the ports and harbours of North-East England. Many of these seamen also served on the warships that were built and maintained in the shipyards of the region. One wonders how many local seamen circumnavigated the globe with Anson or Cook and fought under Nelson at the Battle of Trafalgar. In a few cases the names of some of these seamen have survived. Jack Crawford of Sunderland, hero of the Battle of Camperdown, received a pension for life for services to his country. Less well known, but no less famous to their nautical contemporaries, were Thomas Allen of Hartley in Northumberland, John Scrivener of North Shields and James Melvin who came from Sunderland. These men were elected as delegates of the fleet during the famous mutiny at Spithead in 1797. The mutiny began a new era in the history of the Royal Navy and collier seamen from the North-East contributed decisively to its organization and success.

At a time when Britain trusted to the Navy and the skills of her merchant seamen, the events of 1797 were, perhaps, the clearest demonstration of the crucial relationship between the two. In the age of the sailing ship, fishermen, river workers and merchant seamen possessed, to use a modern phrase, transferable skills, which sustained the Navy in time of war. The Merchant Navy memorial at South Shields commemorates the sacrifice of a subsequent generation of seamen in the wars of a later age. This close and sometimes tense relationship between the Admiralty and the merchant service was evident as recently as the Falklands War.

During the numerous wars of the late eighteenth and early nineteenth centuries, the relationship between the Navy and the merchant service manifested itself in a number of ways, notably in the activities of the *Press Gang* and the commissions provided to *Privateers*. This collection of essays, two of them reprinted from *The Mariners Mirror* and three published here for the first time, explore these aspects of maritime history with particular reference to North-East England.

Pressing seamen for service in the Navy was an age old practice and its legality was hardly disputed even by those who were its principal victims. During the eighteenth century the Impress Service employed hundreds of officers and men. Press gangs were almost a permanent feature of large port towns like Newcastle, Shields and Sunderland. However, despite the numerous arguments which were raised in its defence, impressment was not the most effective way of 'recruiting' seamen for service in the Navy, and it remained a matter of considerable controversy.

The first essay in this volume, *The Mutiny in the James and Thomas* by Dr. N.A.M. Rodger, was originally published in *The Mariners Mirror*, Volume 70 (1984). It describes one of the violent incidents which sometimes occurred, when pressed seamen challenged the right of their captors to hold them against their will.

An acknowledged expert on many aspects of the character and administration of the Royal Navy during the eighteenth century, Dr. Rodger is the author of *The Wooden World: An Anatomy of the Georgian Navy* (Collins, 1986). He was formerly an Assistant Keeper at the Public Record Office and is currently the Anderson Fellow of the National Maritime Museum, Greenwich.

Confrontation is one of the central themes of the second paper, *The Noble Ann Affair, 1779*, written by the editor. It explains the troubled relationship between one group of protected seamen, the Greenland whalermen, and the Navy. Violent incidents between protected seamen and the press gang seem to have occurred with greater regularity than amongst other categories of mariners. For this reason, the Admiralty was generally reluctant to instigate a 'press from protections' and resorted to them only when the demand for seamen reached a critical level. The subsequent experience of the Greenlanders pressed from the *Noble Ann* and other local whalers, during the summer of 1779, makes an interesting case study. Moreover, it reveals that the Admiralty appeared just as ready to restore the freedom of protected seamen as they were to curb the seamen's liberty in the first place.

Professor McCord's paper, *The Impress Service in North-East England during the Napoleonic War*, was first published in *The Mariners Mirror*, Volume 54 (1968). It examines the character and responsibilities of the Regulating Officers of the Impress Service and describes the administrative structure that underpinned the activities of the press gang. Relations between merchant seamen and the Impress Service were not always as hostile as some accounts suggest. The opportunity to republish one of Professor McCord's numerous papers will be widely welcomed. His recent award of an Honorary Doctorate of the Open University was a just acknowledgement of Professor McCord's wide ranging contribution to the development of interest in the history of the region.

The penultimate essay in this volume switches the emphasis to a lesser known, but no less important facet of the relationship between the Admiralty and the merchant service—*Privateering*. Dr. Davíd J. Starkey is currently Leverhulme Research Fellow in British Maritime History at the University of Exeter. He is a principal authority on British privateering during the eighteenth century and is widely published in Britain and America. Dr. Starkey's *British Privateering Enterprise in the Eighteenth Century* (Exeter University Press, 1990) has considerably extended our understanding of the economic and military significance of British privateering. Dr. Starkey's, *The Origins and Regulation of Eighteenth Century British Privateering* is published here for the first time. It explains the legal framework which constrained the activities of private ships of war and the procedures which governed the issue of letters of marque and the taking of prizes. Reference is also made to the ways in which the High Court of Admiralty sought to control some of the abuses attributed to the activities of privateers. Readers will discover that some of the letters of marque commissioned in the North-East occasionally fell foul of Admiralty regulations as well.

The final essay in this volume and the second to be contributed by the editor, *Make your Fortune my Boys! and Drub the Dutch—Privateering and the North-East Coast in the later Eighteenth Century*, explores a fascinating but hitherto under-researched aspect of local maritime history. As a survey of privateering activity between the Tees and the Tweed, it examines both the offensive and defensive manifestations of privateering. The peak years of offensive privateering from local ports came during the American War of Independence when a number of successful privateers were fitted out on the river Tyne and at Berwick. However, the years between 1776 and 1783 also represented a period in which enemy privateers were active off the coast of North-East England as well. The exploits of...'the notorious English pirate'...Daniel Fall and the American naval hero, John Paul Jones, were well known to local maritime communities. Enemy privateering carried the sea war close to the ports and river estuaries of the region. In August 1781 the presence of two privateers near Seaton Sluice prompted...

> 60 of the housekeepers of Hartley [to] form themselves into a company for the defence of Sir John Hussey Delaval's works, and of the ships in his harbour...and immediately began to learn the use of their firelocks...[*Newcastle Courant*, 4 August 1781].

The editor would particularly wish to acknowledge the help and cooperation of the other contributors who have allowed their work to be published in this form, and to Dr. Michael Duffy, Hon. Editor *The Mariners Mirror*, for permission to republish the papers by Dr. Rodger and Professor McCord. The Historical Association and the Bewick Press provided the financial support which made the whole thing possible. Special thanks are also due to Pat Barrow for her word processing skills and meticulous attention to detail in the preparation of the camera copy. Adrian Osler, Keeper of Maritime History, Tyne-Wear Museums supported the publication with helpful suggestions and expert guidance with the illustrations. Ray Rutherford produced a striking cover design at short notice with scant resources. Thanks are also due to my wife Val whose dedication to the needs of a young family in a sometimes chaotic household, released the time which enabled me to complete my own contributions to this volume.

The book is dedicated to the memory of John P. Middleton, formerly a lecturer at Newcastle College, who died in 1992. John was a man of the sea and is sadly missed by all of us who admired his capacity for calm in the midst of a storm.

Tony Barrow
Newcastle College
May 1993

THE MUTINY IN THE *JAMES AND THOMAS*

by N.A.M. Rodger

The business of pressing men for the Navy during the eighteenth century, contrary to the popular mythology, was for the most part a humdrum affair, distasteful to all concerned, but seldom marked by violence. When fighting did occur, the hostilities were almost always begun by deserters desperate not to be recaptured. It is arguable that in this respect at least the Navy's policy of awarding heavy deterrent sentences to a tiny minority of deserters while quietly allowing the rest to go unpunished was counter-productive, in that it persuaded deserters to risk anything rather than be recaptured, even though in reality their chances of being severely punished were very small.[1]

Press officers who were attacked, either at sea where most pressing was done, or on land where the risk of an affray was greater, were in a very difficult position, for if in their defence they killed or injured one of their attackers they were likely to be arrested, imprisoned, or sued for damages, sometimes all three. It was taken for granted that very few courts outside London would return anything like an unbiased verdict in a case against a press officer. Providing, and only providing, that it was satisfied that they had not exceeded their authority, the Admiralty was prepared to defend its officers, if necessary in court, but preferably by forestalling legal action. This could be done by simply posting the accused, and sometimes the witnesses, to a foreign station beyond the reach of the civil power, or the officer could be charged at court martial with the same offence, in the hope that an acquittal there would forestall charges elsewhere. Nevertheless, press officers could be and not infrequently were fined or imprisoned, sometimes for years.[2] Even the Admiralty, which naturally looked more sympathetically on the difficulties faced by its officers, never accepted that the use of weapons was justified in any but the most desperate circumstances—which did not, for example, include the prevention of desertion.[3]

This is the background to a dramatic little affair which occurred in the autumn of 1760. Captain John Bover was in charge of the Impress Service at Newcastle, an energetic young officer, and from time to time he despatched tenders full of newly-raised men to the Nore. These tenders were hired merchantmen, commanded by a lieutenant, with the master and crew found by the owners, and some extra men (often, as in this case, landmen from the press gangs) put on board by Bover to guard the pressed men, who were confined below decks by a large grating shipped over the hatchway, and allowed up in groups for air and exercise. Since tenders were virtually unarmed, they had to be escorted to protect them from privateers, and so it was that at the end of September the *Hornet* sloop, Captain George Johnstone, arrived in the Tyne to convoy to the Nore the *James and Thomas* press tender, commanded by Lieutenant Robert Sax.

Sax had had early and bitter experience of the perils of pressing. In June 1755 when he was a lieutenant of the *Prince George*, Captain Rodney, he had been sent away in the *Princess Augusta* tender to press in the Channel, where he had the misfortune to bring to the *Britannia* merchant ship, inward bound from Leghorn, which opened fire on him. He managed to board and subdue her, but in the process three men were killed. Sax was court-martialled for murder and acquitted, and the bodies were on Hawke's orders thrown overboard well out to sea to avoid an inquest.[4] Nevertheless, Sax was pursued by civil lawsuits for years afterwards, and it is not unreasonable to suppose that the experience had weakened his nerve, and thus contributed to the events which were to follow.

Weakness of nerve was one thing never laid to the charge of Captain Johnstone. Vigorous, incisive, and daring to the point of recklessness, he was one of the most striking sea officers of his generation. Hesitation was unknown to him; thought and action were never divided. Swift to appraise a situation, he never troubled to seek advice or permission before he acted. Though eloquent and generous, with charm and much good sense, he was proud, quarrelsome, and wholly without tact. Rules and regulations, fools whether senior officers or otherwise, he ignored. Not surprisingly, his career was turbulent. By 1760 he had already fought two, possibly three duels with brother officers, and had been twice court-martialled.[5] His subsequent political activities as Governor of West Florida and follower of Lord Sandwich made his name well-known outside the Navy, and perhaps demonstrated the weakness of his style when applied to other circumstances than active service in wartime. The hostile judgements of his character which have often been printed, however, come largely from adherents to the good old principle, long since exploded, that any friend of Lord Sandwich was an enemy of mankind.[6]

Few officers in the Service were more ready with tongue and pen than Johnstone, and one cannot do better than recite his narrative[7] of the events which followed:

Hornet Sloop, Yarmouth, October 6th 1760

Sir

Agreeably to the orders I was under to convoy a tender with imprest men from Newcastle to the Nore, I sailed from thence with the *James & Thomas*, commanded by Lieutenant Sax, on September 25th, the wind being then favourable, but before we reached Whitby the same evening, it came to blow directly against us. The great difficulty in entering the port of Tynemouth (continually attended with damage to his Majesty's ships) and the desertion of men whilst in that narrow river, together with the uncertainty of getting to sea again, even with a fair wind, determined me to keep the ocean and trust to fortune for a day or two rather than put back to that disagreeable harbour.

The number of men sent by this tender by far exceeds the usual complement, being 125 on the list, 112 of whom are able seamen, and the best-proportioned men I have seen in my lifetime. For this reason, on the day I left Shields, as soon as I was clear of the ships which surrounded us, I desired Mr. Sax to send on board the *Hornet* 18 of the most mutinous — and 18 men were accordingly sent, but it appears since they were not of the most mutinous, nor such as Lieutenant Sax designed. He says this was owing to Lieutenant Yeomans, who was ordered to assist in transporting them and in the confusion of departing sent others whom Mr. Sax did not intend should have come. This number of 18 so distinguished was as many as I thought the circumstances would require (still expecting a fair wind), or indeed as I conceived I could in justice to the *Hornet's* crew take on board.

On the 27th at 12 at night it began to blow very fresh and the hawser broke wherewith we were towing the tender. From this time, it seems, the imprest men in the tender became extremely troublesome, and at 7 in the morning Mr. Sax made the signal of distress. I immediately went on board the tender, though it blew extremely hard, where I found the imprest men in a violent uproar, threatening to scuttle the ship, and actually tearing up the platform. I thought it my duty to enquire if they had any cause of complaint which it was in my power to remedy; whether they had sufficient room and air and cleanliness, and offering to take any who were willing to go on board the *Hornet*, and some I called by name. To all these questions, which were put extremely distinctly, they answered only by indeterminate reproach and abuse. But that nothing still might be wanting to render their behaviour more inexcusable in case of an insurrection. I endeavoured to show them that their sufferings were in common with the class of life into which they had entered; that the very aversion they showed evinced the necessity of impressing; that they could only blame the constitution of their country which had provided no other effectual method of procuring seamen for his Majesty's service; that it could be no pleasure to the officer employed, however determined he might be to perform his duty; but that now they were fairly imprest and borne for wages and under a pendant the law of the land was clear and express against any disobedient act they might commit, as well as the civil law and the law of nature in self defence and preservation, in case they offered at any means tending to destroy the vessel. I must do them the justice to acknowledge, though I spoke through a trumpet, that I believe not one heard three words of the matter, the tumult was so great. Upon this I was resolved to bear up for Tynemouth, but first thought it proper to send on board the tender a reinforcement of six men with the Master of the *Hornet*, a man whom I could depend on; but before he put off from the side Lieutenant Sax hailed and informed me he had been obliged to fire on the imprest men in the hold, where one was killed and two wounded. I immediately desired the Master to send the wounded men on board, thinking this would have quelled the matter, but with strict orders to Lieutenant Sax in case it had not that effect that he should not be in the least daunted by any consequences which their fatal obstinacy might produce, and since he had begun, to continue firm to his purpose. The boat returned desiring I would come on board, but as I saw no good purpose this could effect, and being uncertain of my own crew, 30 of whom are impressed besides the 18 I had from the tender, I resolved to abide by my station, that on every alternative I might command;

but sent the Gunner, another very worthy officer, with three more hands and the boat's crew, and made the signal to bear up for Tynemouth. Soon after the boat got on board the tender Lieutenant Sax, contrary to my express command often repeated, and the earnest advice of my Master, permitted the imprest men to come upon deck—nay, he was so infatuated that it appears he was the very person who put the ladder down himself, and immediately with all the officers betook themselves to the boat. The imprest men instantly took possession of the tender, and directed her with all the sail they could crowd towards Whitby, striking the pendant. The *Hornet* had by this time got a good way ahead in the course to Newcastle, when she perceived the boat cast off and guessed what had happened. The sea ran very high. I determined first to take up the boat then pursue the tender, which we did with all the sail we could crowd, and came alongside of her near Whitby. Talking to people in that situation always supposes weakness, or at least give such a prepossession. For that reason I did not hail the tender but ordered one shot to be fired, which producing no sign of obedience, and being within three miles of the shore, I ordered the guns to fired as fast as possible. After the second broadside they called for quarter and tacked from the shore. I sent the boat on board with the Master and Surgeon of the *Hornet* and the Master of the tender, but their passions had not as yet subsided sufficiently, and they insisted in keeping upon deck and gloried in what they had done. One man was killed, one dangerously wounded, six severely and four slightly. In this sad situation, where every alternative was so disagreeable, I came to the following resolution, but first I continued sending messages backwards and forwards until I had drawn all our own officers and people from the tender, and then sent the boat manned with some of the imprest men I had on board, with a very sensible sober fellow amongst them to carry the enclosed terms (as near as I can recollect for I had not time to take a copy) and at the same time engaged him to sow divisions amongst them.

Johnstone's terms were these:

1st. That you shall send on board his Majesty's sloop *Hornet* the four following persons as hostages for your good behaviour, viz: Peter Wall, Thomas Soppett, George Mainprize and James Donaldson.

2nd. That the rest shall return quietly and peaceably to the hold in the manner I received you, and submit to the orders of the officers I shall appoint to take charge of his Majesty's tender.

3rd. That you shall immediately hoist his Majesty's pendant.

4th. If these terms are accepted I promise upon my honour you shall receive all the good usage your situation will admit of, and that as far as my interest can extend none shall be punished for this at a court martial.

5th. If these terms are refused Captain Johnstone will consider you as pirates and treat you as such.

6th. Captain Johnstone advises the more sober to consider what blood they are drawing on their head, and not to be led away by the ridiculous rashness of a few, since they must all stand equally involved by the last offer, vis:

7th. Captain Johnstone invites any who are willing to come on board the *Hornet* and begs and requests they will send the wounded.

This scheme succeeded and the terms were accepted. Everything was quiet, I showed no resentment or distinction, and took particular care of the wounded. I thought after the unaccountable behaviour of Lieutenant Sax he was not to be trusted with such a command again, and therefore I appointed John McLaurin the Master of the *Hornet* to command the tender—a person whom I beg leave in justice to the Service to recommend to their Lordships, as well for his services on this occasion as for diligence, capacity and resolution on every other service. His great ambition is to be a lieutenant, for which he has passed, and I believe no man is fitter for the trust. I must likewise in justice to Lieutenant Sax acknowledge his situation admits of mitigating circumstances, and that he seems to me to have totally lost his senses after the shock of firing at the people in the hold, one of whom he conceived was dead, but there were only two wounded. It was a cruel dilemma he was reduced to, and as he has been once tried before for killing men in a Turkey ship, and besides harrassed by the civil law, I would hope it might at least save his bread.

After the mutiny we met with extreme bad weather, but as I foresaw perplexing consequences in returning to Newcastle within the civil jurisdiction, I chose rather to keep the sea. This gave the men in the tender time to form a second scheme for their escape. They had got knives and coarser instruments when they had possession of the ship, and had actually cut through two-thirds of the bulkhead when they were discovered. The resolution of Mr. McLaurin, and timely assistance, prevented them from executing their desperate scheme, when all were to have been murdered, so that we arrived safe in Yarmouth Roads. Ten men who were on bond[8] to go with the tender to the Nore, and in consequence had the liberty of the deck, were the great promoters of the scheme for destroying the tender, because if that was done their bonds would be discharged. I found on going on board and demanding those who had been at work on the bulkheads and explaining their breach of agreement, that a second mutiny was arising, and finding their prejudices and their union to be too strongly rivetted to be broke when together. I craved the assistance of Captain Bishop, who agreed to receive one half into his tender. Two of the ringleaders and two of the accessory bondsmen I have put in irons. So great a body of men feel their own force and add fury to each other's passion. As many are deserters, and all the others in a desperate condition, in order to prevent further bloodshed I have applied to Captain Bishop for his tender to conduct part of them to the Nore, which he has readily acquiesced in if none of his Majesty's ships should pass before.

I presume this will call for an enquiry, and if it is their Lordships' opinion, beg they will be pleased to order me a court martial as soon as we can determine whether the other man dangerously wounded shall die or survive.

I must crave forgiveness for taking up so much of their Lordships' time, but as it is a matter which I apprehend will come before a court martial, I thought it necessary to inform their Lordships of every circumstance as fully as I could.

On 14 October he wrote from the Nore to complete the story:

This afternoon his Majesty's sloop *Hornet* arrived here with the *James & Thomas* and the *Bird* tenders under convoy, bringing 128 imprest men.

In my last letter from Yarmouth I acquainted their Lordships with my transaction as far as that road, which I conjectured would call for a court martial, and I am now confirmed in my opinion by the advice I have received from an eminent counsellor. I have the pleasure to acquaint their Lordships that it is the opinion of my Surgeon the person dangerously wounded will probably recover, so that I have now to beg their Lordships will be pleased to order a court martial to try me for the murder of George Thompson, mariner, on the 27th September, he being then on board the *James & Thomas* tender at sea off Whitby; and likewise for wilfully and maliciously firing several guns loaded with shot pointed towards the said tender at the time and place aforesaid, whereby John Ramsey, mariner, received a very dangerous wound by a large shot which went entirely through the right shoulder, carrying away in its passage part of the clavicle or colar bone and part of the scapula or blade bone; also John Tollis received a wound by a swivel shot in the upper part of his left arm; also James Donaldson received a wound in the heel. These are all that were wounded severely. I am told that the nearer the words of the charge run to the word of an indictment that it will more effectually prevent any future civil prosecution; but in such a case as this where I am conscious of having done nothing more than my duty, and that in the most prudent manner, I would gladly hope their Lordships will take the best method to screen me from further litigation and trouble.

One week after they anchored at the Nore, Lieutenant Sax, broken by the experience, asked leave to resign his commission.[9] Johnstone duly got his court martial[10] and acquittal, and he continued to command the *Hornet*. In December 1761 he was lucky enough to bring a French privateer prize to Lisbon just as the news arrived that Spain had declared war.[11] Realizing the importance of getting information to the West Indies as fast as possible, on his own authority he put John McLaurin in command of the prize and despatched him to Rodney, while he himself sailed for England. McLaurin made a remarkably fast passage[12] and Rodney was warned in time to seize the initiative (and many valuable prizes) in the Caribbean. For these services Johnstone was made post, and McLaurin received £200.[13] More importantly for his ambitions, he must have made an impression on Rodney, though it took a few years to bring results. In April 1779 McLaurin became Third Lieutenant of the *Romney* in which Johnstone was flying his broad pendant, and in June of the following year, less than fourteen months after he had received his first commission, he was made post by Rodney into his flagship the *Princess Royal*[14]—a long wait, but in the end a rise as rapid as any in the history of the Service.

The careers of McLaurin and Johnstone are almost perfect examples of the opportunities available to able and ambitious young men in the eighteenth-century Navy, and of how they were actually to be exploited. Both Scots, though from very different social backgrounds,[15] both became followers of that brilliant and singular officer Captain Augustus Hervey,[16] and their mutual dependence as follower and leader was typical of the ties which linked the careers of officers throughout the service.

In this as well as other ways, the *James & Thomas* affair, though in itself quite as untypical of the working of the impress service as Johnstone and Sax were untypical of the general run of sea officers, casts an interesting light on several aspects of the life of the Navy in the mid-eighteenth century.

Reprinted by permission of the Editor, *The Mariners Mirror*

Note

Since this article was published in 1984 a number of publications have increased our knowledge of the subject and period. George Johnstone now has a biography by Robin F.A. Fabel, *Bombast and Broadsides, The Lives of George Johnstone*, (Tuscaloosa, 1987), though it passes briefly over his early career and adds little on the *James & Thomas* affair. On impressment and naval recruitment in general the reader may now consult N.A.M. Rodger, *The Wooden World: An Anatomy of the Georgian Navy* (London, 1986), also 'Stragglers and Deserters from the Royal Navy during the Seven Years' War', *Bulletin of the Institute of Historical Research*, LVII (1984) pp.56-79. An important study is David J. Starkey, 'War and the Market for Seafarers in Britain, 1736-1792', in Lewis R. Fischer & Helge W. Nordvik, eds., *Shipping and Trade, 1750-1950: Essays in International Maritime Economic History* (Pontefract, 1990) pp.25-42.

On one point the article requires correction: Johnstone was never a political follower of Lord Sandwich. He returned from America in 1778 a powerful orator and a valuable potential ally whom Lord North's administration was glad to recruit, but he had no personal connection with the First Lord of the Admiralty, and his appointment to command the Cape Expedition of 1780 was forced by North over Sandwich's protests. The matter is dealt with by Fabel, *Bombast and Broadsides*, pp.130-133 & 144; also by N.A.M. Rodger, *The Insatiable Earl: A Life of John Montagu, Fourth Earl of Sandwich, 1718-1792* (London, 1993), p.283.

N.A.M.R.

May 1993

Notes

1. Stephen Gradish, *The Manning of the British Navy during the Seven Years' War* (London, Royal Historical Society, 1980) p.111, estimates that as many as 40,000 men may have deserted during that war. From (Public Record Office MSS) ADM 12/22 & ADM 1/5294-5302 it can be shown that of these 254 were accused at court martial of desertion, 53 were convicted and sentenced to death (nearly half of them for desertion aggravated by other crimes), and as many as a dozen may actually have been hanged. Gradish, p.111, says five on the basis of Admiralty Minutes, but this takes no account of overseas stations whose commanders in chief could confirm sentences without reference to the Admiralty. I know of at least six men hanged overseas for desertion during this war.
2. Lieutenant Peter Rawlings, a press officer imprisoned for his inability to pay a fine imposed on him in a Bristol court in 1756, was still in prison nine years later, by this time insane, and his wife and children starving. ADM 1/578, Captain Samuel Graves to Philip Stephens, 3/iv/65.
3. ADM 1/5299 f.110. ADM 1/717, Commodore Lachlan Leslie to John Cleveland, 23/i/60.
4. ADM 1/5295 s.d. 14/xi/55. Rodney Papers, PRO 30/20/6, Rodney to Hawke, 2/vi/55.
5. ADM 1/5296 f.169 (National Maritime Museum MS) UPC/2 No. 118. Sir J.K. Laughton in the *Dictionary of National Biography*. Sir Lewis Namier & John Brooke, *The History of Parliament; The House of Commons 1754-1790* (London, H.M.S.O., 1964, 3vv.) II, 684.
6. E.g. John Charnock, *Biographia Navalis* (London, 1794-98, 6vv.) VI, 494; or J.H. Broomfield, 'Lord Sandwich at the Admiralty Board: Politics and the British Navy 1771-1778', *Mariners Mirror* 61 p.8. For Johnstone's friendship with Sandwich see George Martelli, *Jemmy Twitcher* (London, 1962) p.208. It is fair to add that Johnstone's career at sea during the American War was not uniformly successful.
7. ADM 1/1985, quoted by permission of the Controller of H.M.S.O. Spelling and punctuation have been modernized, except for the spelling of the word 'imprest'.
8. Probably 'substitutes', men engaged by others who had been discharged from the Navy on condition of finding able seamen in their places.
9. ADM 1/717, Commodore William Boys to Cleveland, 22/x/60.
10. ADM 1/5299 f.633; it contains much illuminating detail about the affair not included in Johnstone's report of proceedings.
11. Julian Corbett, *England in the Seven Years' War* (London, 1907, 2vv.) II, 232.
12. How fast is uncertain. Corbett (II, 235 n.1.) finds himself unable to confirm or refute Robert Beatson, *Naval and Military Memoirs of Great Britain from 1727 to 1783* (London, 1804, 6vv.) II, 531, who states that McLaurin arrived on 18th January after a passage of twenty-three days. Rodney himself stated in a letter written on 23rd that the news had reached him on 22nd, but in a second letter of the same day he put the date back to 18th (PRO 30/20/8 pp.49 & 50).
13. Beatson and Corbett, *loc. cit.* Corbett is incorrect in stating that they were **both** made post.
14. ADM 6/21 p.541. ADM 6/22 p.306.
15. Johnstone was the son of a baronet and nephew of Lord Elibank. McLaurin's parentage I do not know, but it can hardly have been elevated; he entered the Navy on the lower deck from the merchant service.
16. ADM 107/4 p.210. ADM 107/5 p.109.

THE NOBLE ANN AFFAIR
1779

A CASE STUDY OF IMPRESSMENT DURING THE
AMERICAN REVOLUTIONARY WAR

by Tony Barrow

On July 30, 1779, the *Noble Ann*, Greenland whaler of Newcastle, arrived off Shields bar with the produce of three whales. As the vessel entered the river Tyne it was surrounded by boats from the *Syren*, a new frigate then fitting out at Shields, and boats from the Rendezvous at Shields and several press tenders anchored in the river. The crew of the *Noble Ann* refused to surrender themselves and resisted all attempts by the press gang to stop and board their vessel. The violent confrontation which followed left two men dead and a third seriously wounded, all from the crew of the *Noble Ann*. It was undoubtedly the most serious clash between Greenland seamen and the press gang during the American Revolutionary War. But the *Noble Ann* affair was not an isolated incident. During the second half of the eighteenth century there were at least four other violent incidents when attempts to press the crews of Greenland ships led to death or serious injury amongst the participants.[1] The root causes of these confrontations lay on the one hand, in the special character of the seamen involved, and on the other, in the Admiralty's periodic decisions to instigate a press from protections.

'Greenlanders', as they were known to their nautical contemporaries, were a close knit and well-organised fraternity of seamen with a considerable reputation for toughness and independence. They were included in several categories of mariners entitled to protection from impressment and were, therefore, especially sensitive to the activities of the press gang. The crew of the *Noble Ann* were amongst several hundred 'Greenlanders' pressed from their protections during the summer of 1779 whose subsequent, collective experience, demonstrated that the reality of impressment could be considerably different from the popular mythology that surrounded it. Moreover, the *Noble Ann* case offers historians a useful insight into another element of this popular mythology; the apparent arbitrary nature of impressment at the end of the eighteenth century, and the assumption that once impressed, disability, death or desertion were the only means by which a man might be released from naval service. It is an impression that is in many ways reinforced by the D, DD and R columns of the muster books of eighteenth century warships.[2]

The genesis of the *Noble Ann* affair lay in the crisis which followed Burgoyne's surrender at Saratoga in 1777. The entry of the French into the war on the side of the American colonists in February 1778 and the declaration of Spain in the following year overstretched British resources and threatened to disrupt the management of naval operations. The First Lord of the Admiralty, Earl of Sandwich, was well aware of the implications of the crisis...

> 'out of 50 ships which is in our whole stock at present', he wrote to Lord North, 'only 41 can be said to be in readiness and some men are wanted even for their equipment, the others cannot be got to sea without some extraordinary measures are used for raising seamen'...[3]

The situation deteriorated during the course of the year. In March 1779, a summary of the state of ships of the line in commission, in home waters, showed them to be 5600 seamen and marines short of complement with a little over 2000 men 'disposable' to fill the vacancies.[4] Nor was a shortage in the quantity of seamen the only consideration. The crisis of manning also called for the recruitment of experienced seamen who might bring some quality to the fleet.

Captain Walsingham of the *Thunderer* wrote to the Admiralty on 4 June 1779, criticising the condition of newly recruited seamen...'added to their want of knowledge, they are the poorest dirty vermin that ever came on board a man-o-war'...[5]

Now allowing for the less than objective tone of Walsingham's complaint, it was clear that the fleet needed good seamen as well as more seamen, and the situation called for speedy and effective, if unpalatable and potentially provocative solutions. A general press, to include all protected seamen, was central to the several schemes of recruitment proposed during June 1779. The Admiralty ordered naval officers commanding warships together with those employed on the Impress Service to ignore all the protections it had issued to different categories of mariners, watermen and river workers. But Lord Sandwich was uneasy about the possible repercussions of the policy and called for Parliamentary sanction. An Act of Indemnity suspending all Admiralty protections for a limited period was duly passed,[6] but only after a 'hot press' had already begun. Press gangs up and down the country made a clean sweep of all available men. By early July it was reported that 6500 men had already been impressed in England and Wales.[7]

At sea, some of the earliest victims of the emergency were the crews of whaling vessels returning from their seasonal voyages to the Arctic. The Greenland whalermen had long been recognised as a skilled resource, and they represented just the kind of quality seamen the Admiralty were on the look out for. Few of them could have known about the emergency at home. Only those that touched at Orkney or Shetland, or had the opportunity to speak to fishing boats and vessels that were outward bound into the Atlantic, could have received news of the situation. Armed ships and men-o-war were ordered to cruise off the east coast of Britain to intercept homeward bound whalers and press their crews. The commanders of those ships were no doubt prepared for the likelihood of armed confrontations with the Greenland seamen. As one of the Newcastle newspapers put it at the departure of an armed ship from the river Tyne...

'it is supposed the *Content* is gone in search of the Greenland ships...to press all their hands...She will certainly feel bold with a lamb like adversary!'...[8]

Such was the bad feeling that traditionally existed between the 'Greenlanders' and the Navy by the time of the American War that a violent incident of some kind seemed almost inevitable. Moreover, the situation at Shields was exacerbated by several earlier incidents. In February 1777, 17 impressed seamen succeeded in overpowering their guards on the *Union* tender and carried the vessel out to sea under fire from the guns at Clifford's Fort at Shields and naval tenders anchored in the river. The men made their escape at Scarborough, 60 miles to the south of the river Tyne. Later the same month, Lt. Oakes, the Impress Officer at Shields was responsible for shooting and mortally wounding a seaman in attempting to break up a strike. His action caused so much bitterness amongst the seamen at Shields that...'it was thought scarcely possible for the Lieutenant and his people to escape with their lives'...[9] Lt. Oakes had even acquired something of a national reputation as the officer involved in the celebrated Duncan case.[10] Oakes was one of a number of officers directly involved in the *Noble Ann* affair, and the legacy of his actions made it especially difficult for other naval officers hoping to recruit seamen at Shields. One such officer, Edmund Dod, became a key player in the affair.

Dod had been promoted captain in May 1779 and was appointed to command the *Syren*, a new frigate completing construction at Hurry's dockyard at Howdonpans. Dod hoped to man the *Syren* on Tyneside, but despite recruitment advertisements in the Newcastle newspapers and his considerable reputation as a humane and courageous sea officer, he found it difficult to raise a sufficient number of volunteers. He expressed his concern at...'the small prospect I have of raising men at Newcastle and Shields'..., in a letter to the Admiralty only a week after his arrival on Tyneside. Dod asked for a naval cutter or press tender...'to enable me to press the men out of the ships before they come to Shields or I shall find it a difficulty to man the *Syren*'...[11]

As the senior naval officer on Tyneside, Dod had received orders to instruct armed ships to cruise off the east coast for the Greenland whalers and he sent the *Terrible*, cutter, to patrol off the Northumberland coast. The crew of the *Adamant* of Whitby appear to have been amongst the earliest victims of the emergency, they were impressed within sight of their home port on 4 July.[12] Soon afterwards, the crews of several Leith and Dunbar ships were pressed when their vessels were intercepted and boarded at the entrance to the Firth of Forth.[13] At the end of July a number of the

London whalers were also stopped by armed ships off the North-East coast.[14] Two of the Newcastle whalers, the *Kitty* and the *Noble Ann* arrived off the Tyne on 30 July. The *Kitty's* men, clearly aware of the danger they were in, managed to get ashore on the Northumberland coast and avoided a confrontation with the press gang at Shields. The crew of the *Noble Ann* may well have planned to do the same, but they were unable to get close enough inshore before they attracted the attentions of the Navy. Dod's correspondence remains the most vivid and detailed description of the events that followed.

'At daylight this morning a Greenland brig anchored without this bar and landed all her men (to the amount of thirty), another of them, the barque *Noble Ann* had not time to get near enough before I sent all the boats belonging to the *Syren* the tender and the Rendezvous at Shields and attempted to impress the men, but they called to the boats to keep off or they would fire into them and sink them, the Tompions were out of the guns (six carriage guns) and they were armed with blunderbusses and long fish knives, like scythes, fastened to the end of half pikes, they said they were determined to be cut in pieces before they would suffer themselves to be impressed, when I found them so desperate I ordered the *Speedwell* and the *Union* tender to get ready and go out to her in order to board her, one on each side, but before they could get out, the barque *Noble Ann* came in over the bar and bid defiance to us. I manned and armed the boats and went myself in the *Syren's* pinnace, and spoke to them, I offered them the Bounties and every encouragement usually given, particularly the choice of ships they wished to serve on board. I told them of the Suspension Act of Parliament and of the French and Spanish War, and the present situation of Public Affairs, in short I said everything I could think of to induce [sic] them to enter or surrender themselves quietly, but their answer was, they were determined to die rather than be taken and that they would destroy every man that should attempt to come on board; the shores on both sides were lined with people who insulted me and all the Officers with me, in the grossest manner. Thus situated and finding they had cut their cable, and had made sail, to run out of the harbour to sea and the wind being fair for the purpose, I gave orders for the tenders to board her, but she passed them, and in passing gave the most abusive language to us; the officer in the *Union* called to me repeatedly to let them fire, I at last ordered them to fire to bring them to, but unfortunately three men were wounded and one of these so dangerously that he is passed all hopes of recovery, another so badly that he has been trapanned [sic]...I am now on board the *Syren* where I shall remain until I know their lordship's pleasure how I am to act on this melancholy occasion'.[15]

Dod's persistence finally won the day and the whalermen on board the *Noble Ann* eventually surrendered themselves to him. But Dod now found himself in a difficult and dangerous legal situation. John Bover, the Regulating Captain at Newcastle advised Dod to get away from Shields as soon as possible.

'I this moment came from the Solicitor-General' wrote Bover, '(and) he gives it as his opinion that you are in the utmost danger of your life if you stay at Shields a single day...and his reasons are these: If any information whatever is given to the Grand-Jury, at these Assizes, that you gave the order to fire (and unhappily it is too well known already you did do it) he is clear that you will immediately be taken up, tried and condemned for wilful murder...from the noise and clamour the unhappy event occasions here the judge may himself order you to be taken up'...[16]

Dod accepted Bover's advice and left Shields in the early hours of 2 August.

Thomas Smith, one of the seamen wounded in the affray, died the same night. On the following day, a coroners jury at Newcastle returned a verdict of 'feloniously murdered by persons unknown'. When Dod heard the news he was already at Deal. He took ship for Ostend on the following day where he remained for almost three weeks. The other seaman wounded on 30 July also died several days later and a coroners jury at North Shields brought in precisely the same verdict. Dod was advised that unless he could provide witnesses who would testify that his actions had been manslaughter and not murder, he had better...'Keep out of the way at present'...[17] Dod eventually returned from Ostend at the end of August and hastened to Sheerness where he resumed command of the *Syren* on 5 September.

The public outcry caused by the *Noble Ann* case rumbled on at Newcastle and Shields for several weeks...

'We do not hear that any further inquiry is making after the perpetrators of the late murders of the seamen belonging to the *Noble Ann* in Shields harbour. The infamous deed is to be buried in the mists of time like the massacre in St George's Fields'...[18]

When the *Syren* sailed for the Nore of 25 August she carried over 150 Greenland seamen impressed from half a dozen different whalers. Some of them, principally from the *Noble Ann*, mustered as part of the crew of the *Syren*, the others were carried as supernumaries for delivery to the receiving ship at the Nore. Amongst them were 36 seamen pressed from the crew of another Newcastle ship, the *Priscilla*, which had arrived in the Tyne from the Davis Straits on 21 August. The crew of the *Priscilla*, like the crew of the *Noble Ann* before them, had resisted their impressment and for a time it looked as if another ugly incident with the Greenland seamen might have occurred. But, with the consequences of the *Noble Ann* affair still fresh in their minds, Sir Harry Heron, commander of the *Merchant*, and Lt. Nagle of the *Syren*, adopted a less confrontational stance towards the *Priscilla's* recalcitrant seamen. The log of the *Merchant* provides the clearest picture of the affair...

21 August

'At ½ past ten came in the *Priscilla* Greenland ship when all the boats of the fleet were sent to press their people. They took to their arms and would not suffer the boats to come alongside upon which we slipped our moorings, weighed the anchor and followed them up the river. At 12 pm came to an anchor and secured with her...the people then took to their close quarters. Sent the *Queen* to lay on the other side in order to press them without doing any damage'.

22 August

'At 9 am finding the Greenland men would not submit...but they were not so seditious as the evening before, broke open their close quarters and took out of her 36 men'...[19]

An analysis of the subsequent service of many of these Greenland seamen demonstrates not only that the Admiralty stuck closely to the letter of the law, but also, that the experience of impressment had no long term effect upon their careers. The majority of the men, 120 in total, were discharged from the *Syren* into the *Conquestador*, the receiving ship at the Nore. A further ten men were sent on board the *Scarborough*. Most of the men impressed from the crew of the *Noble Ann* remained with the *Syren*.[20] Figure 1 summarises their subsequent service and shows that the majority of them were discharged in time to proceed to the Whale Fishery in 1780. Only five of the seamen impressed from the *Noble Ann* remained with the *Syren* for more than a year. Michael Rippon and Thomas Morrison mustered with the ship as long as Dod remained in command of it, but after his appointment to another frigate, the *Lizard*, in January 1781, Rippon and Morrison ran from the ship at Portsmouth. They were the only seamen who appear to have done so. Roberts, Kell and Scotland remained with the *Syren* until she was wrecked on the Sussex coast in 1781. It is not known if they survived the shipwreck.[21]

The surviving muster rolls of many Greenland ships at Shields and Whitby reveal the names of whalermen who had been impressed during the summer emergency of 1779. George Wilson and Francis Allely from the crew of the *Noble Ann*, mustered as harpooners in the *Priscilla* after 1782 together with a number of other seamen who had been impressed from that ship in August 1779.[22] Thomas Forster, another seaman who had been impressed during the incident involving the crew of the *Priscilla*, mustered as a harpooner of the *Jenny's Adventure* and *Nautilus*, both of Whitby, between 1784 and 1788.[23] There are numerous other examples, and that of Thomas Banks is especially interesting. Banks was impressed from the crew of the *Addison* of Whitby by the *Content* armed ship during 17 August 1779 and delivered on board the *Syren*. He was discharged from the *Syren* on 28 January 1780 and reached Whitby in time to muster as a seaman on the *Addison* for her voyage to the Davis Straits. By 1784 he was mate of the *Friendship*, also of Whitby, and was promoted to command the *Prospect* in 1786.[24] Two other seamen impressed at the same time as Banks, Robert Burley and Bartholomew Robson also assumed command of whaleships at Whitby and Shields in 1785 and 1786.[25] Michael Rippon, the seaman who had deserted from the *Syren*, and Edward Stove who had been pressed from the *Priscilla*, mustered together as boatsteerers on the *Euretta* of Shields in 1798, almost twenty years after their association with the *Noble Ann* affair.[26]

Figure 1. **Subsequent experience of 25 Greenland seamen impressed from the crew of the** *Noble Ann*

Name	Age	Birth	Position	Rating and subsequent service
George Wilson	24	Newcastle	HPR	Armourer-*SYREN* -d.Deal 16/5/1780
Robert Snowball	-	-	HPR	d.*SYREN* into *CONQUESTADOR* 11/9/1779 d.*CONQUESTADOR* into *ORFORD* (HS) 6/10/1779 d.ADM ORDERS 28/1/1780
John Wright	19	Yarmouth	HPR	AB -*SYREN* -d.ADM ORDERS 28/1/1780
James Wheeler	-	-	HPR	d.*SYREN* into *CONQUESTADOR* 11/9/1779 d.*CONQUESTADOR* into *ORFORD* (HS) 12/10/1779 d.ADM ORDERS 28/1/1780
Thomas Curry	26	Yarmouth	BST	O.S.-*SYREN* -d.ADM ORDERS 28/1/1780
Francis Catchfall	24	Sunderland	BST	AB -*SYREN* -d.into *MONTAGUE* 11/9/1779
William Black	28	Shields	BST	AB -*SYREN* -d.ADM ORDERS 28/1/1780
Edward Hewison	25	Shields	HPR	AB -*SYREN* -d.ADM ORDERS 4/3/1780
John Francis	35	Shields	BST	AB -*SYREN* -d.ADM ORDERS 28/1/1780
John Nicholson	-	-	BST	AB -*SYREN* -d.ADM ORDERS 28/1/1780
Robert Softley	25	Sunderland	LMG	Yeoman of Sheets -*SYREN* -d.ADM ORDERS 28/1/1780
William Duffield	28	Shields	LMG	AB -*SYREN* -d.ADM ORDERS 28/1/1780
James Dixon	24	Leicester	LMG	AB -*SYREN* -d.ADM ORDERS 28/1/1780
Francis Allely	21	Newcastle	LMG	AB -*SYREN* -d.ADM ORDERS 28/1/1780
James Brelsford	22	Newcastle	LMG	AB -*SYREN* -d.ADM ORDERS 28/1/1780
Thomas Morrison	21	Norwich	Seaman	OS -*SYREN* Run at Portsmouth 14/1/1781
John Kell	-	-	Seaman	OS -*SYREN* -remained
James Scotland	-	-	Seaman	OS -*SYREN* -remained
Michael Rippon	20	Sunderland	Seaman	AB -*SYREN* Run at Portsmouth 14/1/1781
John Law	-	-	Seaman	OS -*SYREN* -d. into *CONQUESTADOR* 11/9/1779 d.ADM ORDERS 28/1/1780
James Roberts	-	-	APP	-*SYREN* -remained
Richard Horsley	-	-	Seaman	OS -*SYREN* -d. into *CONQUESTADOR* 11/9/1779 d.ADM ORDERS 28/1/1780
John Brown	-	-	Seaman	OS -*SYREN* -d.ADM ORDERS 28/1/1780
Thomas Fleming	-	-	Seaman	OS -*SYREN* -d.ADM ORDERS 28/1/1780
Jonathan Sadler	25	Sunderland	Seaman	AB -*SYREN* -d.ADM ORDERS 28/1/1780

Sources: PRO BT 98/129 No.125 Muster roll of the *Noble Ann*
PRO ADM 36/9738 Muster book of the *SYREN*
PRO ADM 36/8162 Muster book of the *CONQUESTADOR*

Abbreviations:
HPR = Harpooner
BST = Boatsteerer
LMG = Linemanager
d. = discharged
HS = Hospital Ship

Notes:
1. Dod stated in the log of the *SYREN* that he had impressed 32 seamen from the *Noble Ann* of whom 25 were mustered to the *SYREN*.
2. Although Thomas Fleming and Jonathan Sadler appear to have been impressed from the crew of the *Noble Ann* their names do not appear on the muster of that ship.

The crisis of manning occasioned by the outbreak of the French Wars in 1793 saw a revival of the activities of the press gangs and Greenland seamen became targets for impressment once again. The crews of homeward bound whalers were especially vulnerable to the attentions of patrolling warships, just as they had been during the summer of 1779 and the resulting confrontations had a familiar ring. In July 1794 the *Sarah and Elizabeth* of Hull was intercepted off St. Abbs Head by the frigate *Aurora* (Captain William Essington), who intended to press men from her crew. The Greenland seamen took to their close quarters determined to resist the attempt. In the resulting confrontation one man was killed and several others wounded. An inquest was held on the dead man at Hull and the jury found Essington guilty of wilful murder. On this occasion the Admiralty proved more supportive to Essington that it had to Dod. They kept him at sea so that he could not be arrested and tried. Essington was then posted to the Indian Ocean, and, like Dod before him, he was never called to answer charges.[27] There were further confrontations between Greenlanders and the press gang in 1798, 1804 and 1807.[28] It was incidents such as these that contributed to the widespread notoriety that was popularly attached to the activities of press gangs during the late eighteenth and early nineteenth centuries. However, even though violent confrontations involving Greenland seamen certainly occurred with greater regularity than they did amongst other categories of seamen, they do not appear to have had any lasting effect upon the men involved with them. For its part the Admiralty usually honoured its commitments to protected seamen. The crew of the *Sarah and Elizabeth* were released soon after their arrival at the Nore,[29] just as the crew of the *Noble Ann*, the *Priscilla* and the Whitby ships had been released when the period of suspension of their protections had expired. Moreover, despite the public furore that surrounded the *Noble Ann* affair, and the immediate threat it seemed to pose to the career of the senior naval officer involved, Edmund Dod, it proved to have no lasting effect upon him either. After serving only eighteen months as captain of the *Syren*, Dod was posted to command another frigate, the *Lizard*, which sailed for the West Indies as part of the squadron dispatched there under Sir Samuel Hood in 1781. Dod distinguished himself in several actions against the French in the Leeward Islands and was mentioned in dispatches.[30] Thereafter his naval career followed a familiar pattern of promotion to the command of larger and larger warships. Soon after the outbreak of the French Wars, Dod was posted to command the *Atlas*, a 2nd rate of 90 guns. He became a Rear-Admiral in 1797 and eventually reached the rank of Admiral of the White in 1810.[31]

Edmund Dod died at his home in Exeter, aged 81 in December 1815 'a gentleman of great respectability'.[32]

Notes

1. These were at Newcastle in August 1756; during attempts to press the crew of the *Golden Lyon*, Liverpool whaler, in July 1759; and in relation to the Hull whalers, *Sarah and Elizabeth* in July 1794 and *Blenheim* in July 1798.
2. Discharged, Discharged Dead and Run.
3. Lord Sandwich to Lord North, 6 March 1778. Sandwich Papers, Volume I. p.350.
4. Sandwich Papers, Volume III, p.4.
5. *Ibid.*
6. 19 Geo III c.75. An Act for Removing Certain Difficulties with Respect to the More Speedy and Effectual Manning of HM Navy, for a Limited Time. The Act suspended the protections issued to Greenland seamen for five months computed from 16 June 1779. Seamen in the Coal Trade had their protections suspended for one month only.
7. *Newcastle Courant*, 10 July 1779.
8. *Newcastle Chronicle*, 17 July 1779.
9. Annals of the Northern Counties. Duncan, Vol.IV.
10. Oakes had impressed George Duncan at Shields in 1777, but Duncan claimed that he was exempt on the grounds that he was a freeholder and a voter. The Admiralty referred the case to the Attorney General for his opinion. He concluded that 'I see no reason why men using the sea...should be exempted because they are freeholders...nor did I ever read or hear of such a suggestion'.
11. ADM 1/1708, 19 June 1779.
12. *Newcastle Weekly Chronicle*, 10 July 1779.
13. ADM 51/359.
14. The *Content* intercepted the *Kelso* off Newbiggin Point on 29 July but the Greenlanders mutinied and took to their close quarters. The *Content* put some of her own men on board and escorted the *Kelso* to the Nore where the Greenland seamen were impressed. Two other London whalers, the *Rising Sun* and the *Sea Horse* were brought to off Whitby by the *Queen* armed ship on 31 July. The *Merchant*, another armed ship based at Shields, pressed the crew of the *Exeter* and an unnamed whaler near Flamborough Head of 1 August. See ADM 51/209, 567 and 749.
15. Edmund Dod to Phillip Stephens (Secretary to the Admiralty) 30 July 1779—ADM 1/1708.
16. John Bover to Capt. Edmund Dod, 1 August 1779—ADM 7/300 (where copies of all the correspondence concerning the *Noble Ann* affair can be found).
17. ADM 7/300. Dod seems to have received very little support from the Admiralty even though there had been clear precedents for his actions. In 1778 in the case of Rex v Phillips the officer who gave the order to fire when resistance was made was only convicted of manslaughter. See Lloyd, C. *The British Seaman*, p.168.
18. *Newcastle Chronicle*, 28 August 1779.
19. ADM 51/567.
20. ADM 36/9738 and 8162.
21. Coincidentally the *Noble Ann* was also lost in the same year, sunk at Gibraltar in April 1781. BT 98/130, No.182.
22. PRO BT 98/131 No.199 and BT 98/132 No.112.
23. Muster rolls of the *Jenny's Adventure* (No.212, 1784) and the *Nautilus* (No.282, 1785; No.94, 1786; No.211, 1787); Whitby Literary and Philosophical Society, Whitby Museum.
24. ADM 36/9738 and Muster rolls of the *Addison* (No.44, 1780) and *Friendship* (No.173, 1784). Whitby Museum and GU/TH/237, Tyne & Wear Archives Dept.

25. PRO BT 98/132, No.91 and GU/TH/237.
26. PRO ADM 7/650, 17 September 1798.
27. Gillett E. *The Humber Region at War, 1793-1815*, Humberside Heritage Publications. No.12 (1988). p.5.
28. The most serious of these incidents involved the crew of the Hull whaler *Blenheim* in 1798. In 1804 after an incident involving the crew of a London whaler, the *Ocean*, the owners of the vessel brought a case in the Court of King's Bench which established the illegality of pressing Greenland seamen from their protections. (Pack v MacKay, 12 December 1804.)
29. *Hull Advertiser*, 16 August 1794.
30. Sir Samuel Hood to Earl of Sandwich, 8 February 1782. Sandwich Papers, Vol.IV.
31. Pitcairn-Jones, *Commissioned Sea Officers of the RN, 1660-1815*.
32. *Exeter Flying Post*, 27 December 1815.

THE IMPRESS SERVICE IN NORTH-EAST ENGLAND DURING THE NAPOLEONIC WAR

by Norman McCord

During the short-lived Peace of Amiens, which separated the French Revolutionary from the Napoleonic Wars, the Royal Navy had been reduced in what was to prove an overly optimistic wave of economy. The Impress Service, which had reached a high degree of organization by 1802, was involved in this run-down and had been effectively dismantled.[1] This meant that, when the deteriorating relations with France in the early months of 1803 seemed to involve renewed threat of war and vital need for an expanded navy, the Impress Service had to be built up again in great haste and with inadequate resources.

The north-east ports had always been an important centre for impressment, mainly because their large coastal trades, with their short voyages, presented admirable targets to the press gangs.[2] Not surprisingly then, one of the first new appointments was that of a Regulating Officer for this area. In March 1803 Captain Adam Mackenzie arrived on Tyneside to build up an organization, but in the beginning he had to start from scratch; he arrived alone, without staff, without boats. His first action was to make contact with the civic authorities of Newcastle; until the middle of the century Newcastle occupied a monopolistic position in control of the Tyne harbour and naturally became involved in any matter involving the trade of the port. Mackenzie at first cherished high hopes of the degree of help he might expect from the local authorities, and his first plans envisaged a sweep of the riverside areas in search of seamen, carried out jointly by naval detachments from H.M.S. *Lapwing*, then in the river, and reinforcements provided by Newcastle constables. Captain Skene of *Lapwing* had, however, already warned him that most of the birds had flown;[3] on the first rumour of a press taking place:...'an alarm amongst the seamen, had taken place...by which means most of them were secreted in the country'...

The Mayor of Newcastle was out of town on 18 March, when Mackenzie paid his first visit, but Alderman Foster assured the Regulating Officer that the town would give all possible help, while Alderman Hood offered to provide Mackenzie with a temporary tender to take any seamen caught by the press, in the shape of a brig which he then had lying empty in the harbour. At Newcastle Mackenzie also heard of a naval Lieutenant, Frazier, who was living there on half-pay, and he determined to employ him on the Impress Service in command of the first press gang to be established, since Mackenzie's own orders forbade him to lead a gang in person.[4]

The first sweep on the Tyne duly took place, but few seamen were found because advance information of the impending press had spread, and Mackenzie's somewhat Machiavellian attempt to spread conflicting rumours that no press was to take place was ineffective. However within a week Mackenzie had managed to catch 50 men and incarcerate them in the brig offered by Hood, which for security's sake,[5] was laid alongside *Lapwing*. The brig was far from being an ideal vessel for the job, for when she was taken over she had 'nothing but the wet ballast for the men to lie on'.[6] Mackenzie had to employ a carpenter to build a platform in her, and the first pressed men must have spent some very uncomfortable nights. In any event she would not do to take the first catch to the Fleet base at the Nore, and the Regulating Officer begged the loan of a revenue cutter from the local customs authorities for this purpose.

Lieutenant Frazier proved a distinct disappointment; after only a few days Mackenzie told the Admiralty that he thought little of the man's ability, and in view of the complaint a little later that Frazier suffered from a general want of energy it seems clear enough that he was not the man for this work.[7] The Admiralty responded by providing Mackenzie with 'a more efficient officer' in the person of Lieutenant John Mitchell who arrived in early April, and Frazier was shortly afterwards discharged from active duty. Despite his experience in this matter, Mackenzie added to his staff by enlisting another local half-pay lieutenant, Bounton, although this was done for special reasons which will become clear soon.

Pressure from the Admiralty for a 'hot press' continued, and as Mackenzie became more acquainted with local conditions he was able to institute more efficient arrangements. In late spring and early summer 1803 he was able to spread his activities into new areas, but this expansion was predictably enough punctuated by a series of clashes with the local population. On his arrival Mitchell had been placed in charge of a press gang working in the area around North Shields, and his activities there involved him in a number of stiff fights. One of the most strenuous of these took place on 5 May, when his appearance at the township of Howdon provoked an attack on the press gang by workmen employed in Hurry's dockyard there, who succeeded in wresting a pressed seaman from the gang. The response of the navy was prompt; Mitchell's gang was doubled in size by the summoning of reinforcements and, in response to the Regulating Officer's plea, the Admiralty issued a categorical warning that if such offences were repeated the dockyard workers would have their protections revoked and themselves be exposed to impressment.[8]

The movement of the Impress Service into Sunderland and South Shields also involved serious disturbances. Mackenzie had enlisted Lieutenant Bounton mainly because as a Sunderland man resident in that town he might be supposed to have useful local knowledge. In mid-April then Mackenzie placed Bounton in command of a press gang charged with the task of beginning operations on the Wear. Local reaction was prompt and vigorous, and on 19 April the Regulating Officer reported to the Admiralty that...

'Lieutenant Bounton has this instant come away from Sunderland to inform me, that he durst not attempt to impress at that place last night, as Mobs of hundreds of Seamen, Soldiers and Women, got round the Rendezvous and threatened the lives of himself and People, whether they acted or not'...

Local authority, in the shape of a magistrate and the commander of the local garrison, had declined to give the unfortunate lieutenant any effective help. Mackenzie therefore planned his own counterstroke, and determined to raise every man he could, from his own gangs and the crew of the *Lapwing*, and to force a way into Sunderland for the Impress Service on the next day. The Admiralty at once acted to back him up, passing on to the Home Office for action the complaints about lack of support from local authorities, and telling Mackenzie to let it be known that unless the local magistrates acted to back up the navy, all protections against impressment would be withdrawn from the entire trade of the port—a potent threat.

Mackenzie's prompt retaliation was effective, and on 20 April he could tell the Admiralty that

In my letter of the 19th., I informed you Lieut. Bounton and his Gang had been driven out of Sunderland.

Capt. Skene, myself, all the Gangs under my direction, with several Officers and a strong party of the Lapwing's people went over yesterday.

The seamen all fled, but we were attacked by large Mobs, principally Women, who by throwing things hurt some of the Officers, and rescued several men.

At last the only Magistrate at home in the Town, directed the 30th Regt. to assist in keeping the peace, our own people however had conquered every difficulty without hurting anyone, and I now think the Officer and Gang may go on with their duty.

We took twenty two men, but found only five fit for the Service. Lieut. Bounton is even worse calculated for this Service than Lieut. Frazier. I shall therefore direct them to change Stations till their Lordships are pleased to appoint other officers in their place.

After the severe day's work the men had, I found it necessary to order them some Bread and Beer...which I hope their Lordships, under such circumstances, will not think an improper charge in my disbursements.

Happily the endorsement on this letter at the Admiralty directed that this expenditure should be approved.

In the early part of the war South Shields acted as something of a seamen's refuge, with an organized system of lookouts to give warning of the approach of anyone connected with the Impress Service.[9] While Bounton and Mackenzie were concentrating on the Wear, the newly arrived Mitchell was given this hard nut to crack. He first took his gang over the Tyne to South Shields on 19 April, only to be...[10]

attacked by a Multitude of Pilots and Women, who threw a quantity of Stones and Brickbats at him, they likewise threatened to hew him down with their Spades, which are very dangerous Weapons, they being round and quite Sharp, with Shanks of about Six feet in length, and likewise threatened to Murder him if ever he came back, he applied to the Civil Magistrates but could get no assistance, they being from home.

On 28 April Mitchell tried again, this time supported by a detachment from *Lapwing*. Again there was a very hostile reaction, and on this occasion the only local magistrate available not only positively refused to help the press gang, but deliberately interposed his authority against Mitchell and his men. Once again Mackenzie had to complain to the Admiralty of the uncooperative attitude of the local authorities, and once again the Admiralty invoked the Home Office's aid to bring pressure on the recalcitrant magistrate. The press gang secured an operational footing in South Shields in the summer of 1803 despite these checks, but the town was never a comfortable place in which to carry out its operations. For instance, in mid-August 1806 there were two strenuous but unsuccessful attempts there to rescue pressed men, and the Regulating Officer asked the Admiralty to prosecute some of the ringleaders, including a woman who had thrown a basin and some bricks at a midshipman.[11]

However, by May 1803 Captain Mackenzie could reflect that he had established his forces in all the principal centres of his bailiwick. He now had at his disposal a hired tender, the *Eliza*, to take his victims to the Nore and the Fleet. By the summer of 1803 *Eliza* was being kept busy, for as Napoleon's threat of invasion seemed imminent, pressure from the Admiralty for men mounted still further. For example, *Eliza* sailed with 77 captives on 24 July, and five days later Mackenzie had another 16 men ready, and shipped them off on a warship which happened to call in the Tyne on her way to the Nore. In May the Admiralty had resorted to an emergency measure; Regulating Officers were authorized to make a special press among categories of seamen normally regarded as immune, and for a short while to disregard even protections issued by the Admiralty itself. This 'press from protections' had little success on the Tyne and Wear for it chanced that these harbours had few vessels in at the time. This meagre haul determined Mackenzie to take a step he had been contemplating for some time. The standard warrant given to officers of the Impress Service authorized them to take 'seamen, seafaring men, and others, whose occupations and callings are to work in vessels and boats upon rivers', and the Tyne Regulating Officer had his eye on the river workers of the north-east ports, and particularly on the keelmen, a large body of highly skilled boatmen who manned the sailing barges which brought coal down from the up-river collieries to the colliers waiting in the harbour at the mouth of the river.[12] These men were very desirable game for the Impress Service, but there were dangers in tackling them; they were a notably cohesive and self-confident element in the local population, and believed themselves immune from impressment. It was clear to everyone concerned that to impress the keelmen would bring the whole coal trade to a stop, and therefore bring on to the field not only the keelmen themselves but also their employers and the Corporation of Newcastle. Nevertheless, faced with the navy's critical need for men, the Regulating Officer determined to take the plunge. On 10 May he reported to the Admiralty:[13]

> There are a vast body of fine men in the Keels who were protected by their Lordships. Capt. Skene & myself determined to take as many of the young ones as we could this morning, leaving all Skippers. I beg leave to observe, it is the general opinion here, that nothing will be done on the River, until the Keelmen are again protected, in the mean time we will get all we can.

In fact Mackenzie and his allies seized 53 keelmen. At once all the others downed tools and brought the coal trade of the Tyne to a standstill. The Admiralty's reaction was to approve what Mackenzie had done, but to order him not to take any more keelmen for the time being—probably in anticipation of the type of negotiations which now ensued.

There was at once a flurry of activity among the local vested interests affected. After discussions on the Tyne, one of the coal trade's leading figures, George Dunn, hurried down to London to bring pressure to bear at the Admiralty. He had an interview with two Lords of the Admiralty, Troubridge and Markham, and at last obtained from them an order to the admiral commanding at the Nore for the release of the keelmen. Off he posted to the Nore, arriving there just as H.M.S. *Lapwing* came in with the keelmen on board. While they were being landed a telegraph order from the Admiralty cancelled the order for release which Dunn had obtained, and the unfortunate keelmen were clapped up again. Dunn hastened back to London to try to restore the situation, at first without success. He then fortified himself with the company of two local MPs from the north-east, Sir Matthew Ridley and George Burdon. With this political support he tried again at the Admiralty, now making a definite offer that if a general protection for the Tyne keelmen was given, they would provide a quota of recruits equal to one tenth of the adult keelmen at work—this would have meant the provision of 80 substitutes. The Admiralty demurred, and made difficulties, so the MPs went off to see Addington, the prime minister. Addington had his hands full of troubles, and he ordered the Admiralty to accept the suggested arrangements for raising substitutes. The Admiralty now acquiesced, stipulating only that the quota raised should amount to one prime seaman or two landsmen for each ten keelmen now protected. It is obvious that from the beginning the Admiralty had in fact been looking for some such compromise which would give them a reasonable gain in men without disrupting trade indefinitely.[14]

These negotiations took time, and while they were taking place there was a change on the Tyne; Mackenzie broke a leg and was replaced as Regulating Officer by

Captain William Charleton, who took over in mid-June. His own health was not very good, but Charleton seems to have made an effective head of the Impress Service in the north-east. It was Charleton who supervised the final arrangements with the keelmen, who had to share among themselves the considerable cost of raising 80 substitutes, at a time when the substitute market was invaded by army competition for recruits too. Charleton at once followed up the victory over the Tyne keelmen with two consequent measures. In the first place, the raising of a similar quota from the other watermen of the Tyne was at once insisted upon, and despite grumbling and complaint the wherry-men, coal-trimmers and other river-workers were forced to purchase protection on the same terms as the keelmen. This raised another 27 substitutes. In addition it was obviously necessary to tackle the keelmen on the Wear too. They proved recalcitrant, and it was not until February 1804 that an agreement was reached between the Navy and the Sunderland keelmen; the keelmen had to pay for their obstinacy by accepting worse terms that those of the Tyne, for in addition to the basic 10 per cent quota of substitutes extorted now, the Wear keelmen had to agree to hold a new levy annually, to provide the same quota from men newly joining the trade, or from lads in the trade who attained the age of eighteen and therefore became liable to impressment. This discrepancy in the two compacts with the keelmen was to cause trouble later.

After all these early troubles and problems, the Impress Service in north-east England settled down to a fairly routine existence. When the immediate pressure of the early months of the war was over, the heat of the press diminished somewhat, but even in these quiet years the flow of pressed men to the Fleet from the north-east ports was far from negligible, and two hired tenders were kept busy for most of the rest of the war. Early in 1804, for example, the tender *Lyra* sailed for the Nore with 63 men on 2 January, followed in ten days by her consort *Eliza* with 94 men; on 1 February *Lyra* sailed again with another 66 men, and a week later Charleton had 13 men available when a warship called in the Tyne on her way to the Nore. At a later and still quieter period *Eliza* sailed on 15 May 1806 with 39 men from the Tyne, making first for Leith where she picked up another 30 men before proceeding to the Nore; on 16 July she sailed again from the Tyne with another 40 men.

After the first hectic months the Impress Service in the area stabilized at an establishment of one captain as Regulating Officer, with usually five lieutenants serving under him either in charge of press gangs or commanding the armed naval guard upon the hired tenders. The officers employed on his service were uniformly undistinguished.[15] Charleton was the only one of them to receive significant promotion, and his preferment was scarcely startling; when he was finally superannuated in 1814 he received promotion to rear-admiral, a tribute perhaps rather to his powers of survival than to any notable eminence in his profession. The Impress

Service was not a branch in which ambitious and able officers willingly served, and there was little chance of earning distinction in this work.

The job these men had to do was not always a simple one. There was constant difficulty as to who was liable to impressment and who exempt, producing a whole series of borderline and doubtful cases. The normal practice of the lieutenants commanding the gangs seems to have been to detain a man where there was doubt and leave knotty problems to the Regulating Officer to solve when the captives were brought before him for his decision as to whether or not they should be detained for His Majesty's service. There was no great difficulty in the case of masters of merchant vessels, whose immunity was generally accepted. Other officers of merchant ships were in theory immune from impressment, but in practice two important qualifications to this protection seriously limited its effect, as the mates and the ships' carpenters of the large coasting fleet using the north-east ports soon discovered to their cost. From the beginning the Regulating Officers ruled, and the Admiralty confirmed, that this protection only applied to those officers currently signed on a ship's articles, so that a mate caught after one voyage was over and before signing on for another was regarded as fair game. Many of those caught during the first 'hot press' of 1803 were mates or carpenters who had not signed articles, and yet wrongly supposed themselves immune. Needless to say, a little experience of this interpretation rapidly induced a more punctilious regard for the signing of articles. The second qualification was that the Impress Service limited it for officers other than masters to times when the officer concerned was either actually on board his vessel or on shore explicitly on that ship's business. Mackenzie had openly announced on taking up his appointment that he would follow this practice. There was no redress for the victims in this category, for the courts were notably reluctant to interfere with the prerogative right to impressment during time of war, and in 1811 *habeas corpus* was denied in the case of a ship's carpenter impressed in the Tyne.[16] A few examples will illustrate the way in which the system worked in these years.

On 19 January 1804 George Davidson, mate of a ship lying in the Tyne, was seized by the press gang while drinking in a public house at 9 p.m.; the Regulating Officer confirmed his detention, on the grounds that this could not be construed as ashore on his ship's business, and the Admiralty fully agreed.

The situation could be a good deal more complex. In June 1803 James Watson was a ship's carpenter, classed therefore as an officer and in this case duly signed on for the current voyage. He was nevertheless improperly pressed by men from H.M.S. *Hussar*; after friends complained to the Admiralty his release was ordered, but when he left *Hussar* it was to find that his ship had sailed for the Tyne. Watson made his way to North Shields, feeling safe in possession of a document explaining his case signed by *Hussar*'s captain; however, Mitchell's gang seized him again, on the specious ground that there was an alteration in the date of this certificate—an alteration which *Hussar*'s Captain had in fact made himself. Once again Watson was released from the clutches of the Impress Service when this was explained. He was one of the lucky ones.

A case which did not have such a happy ending was that of Robert Arrowsmith, another ship's carpenter, who was seized on the Tyne at about the same time. His friends and family obtained the intervention of the mayor of Newcastle on his behalf. Not only was he a ship's officer, but he was married with seven children, the oldest of whom was eleven; the mayor reported sadly that the whole family had come on the parish as a result of the father's impressment. Arrowsmith's friends had raised two substitutes to serve in his stead if the navy would let him go. The Admiralty referred the matter to the Regulating Officer, who could find no trace in his records of Arrowsmith's detention, and suggested that he had been pressed by the boats of H.M.S. *Cruizer* acting independently. These exchanges took time, and although eventually the Admiralty ordered the man's release it was too late—the naval vessel on which he was by then serving had sailed for a distant station.

It was well established by statute that no one under eighteen could be impressed, but this exemption could be difficult to apply in practice at a time when personal documentation was a rarity and proof of age not always easy to come by. Regulating Officers could hardly be blamed for refusing to accept a simple assertion of being under age from the individual concerned, but in practice if there was any reasonable proof that a pressed man was under age he would be released. One of the lucky young men in this category was Mark Taught, who in October 1806 was lying in the tender *Lyra* as she awaited a tide on which to sail; a copy of his baptismal record arrived at this eleventh hour and he was discharged. About the same time the Regulating Officer released another youth on receipt of an affidavit from his grandmother declaring him to be under eighteen.

Indeed in general the impression left is that the Impress Service was remarkably punctilious in the way in which its formidable powers were employed. In the period studied here there is not a single clear case of a landsman who had not used the sea being carried into the navy by the Impress Service. The men employed on this service were exposed to severe temptations, and in one instance a midshipman and one or two ratings of the gang based at Sunderland were detected in corruption—accepting bribes to protect certain seamen. The midshipman was at once despatched to the Nore in disgrace, and the ratings discharged from the navy.[17] This situation had developed at a time when the lieutenant in charge on the Wear had been ill for some time. This is the only occasion in the records relevant here where such derelictions come to light.

One reason for this keeping to the rules was undoubtedly the close supervision of the activities of the Impress Service. From the beginning of the war there was a constant stream of enquiry, instruction and complaint issuing from the Admiralty. Upon the devoted head of the Regulating Officer there descended a very large correspondence, for apart from the Admiralty's own independent contribution there was a continuing series of complaints from the Fleet about the quality of some of the men raised, as well as the stream of complaint and pleading from the families and friends of those seized for the Service.

Sometimes political influence could be mobilized on behalf of pressed men, but even this was not necessarily effective. Samuel Dodds was pressed by Lieutenant Frazier at Newcastle, and his detention confirmed by Mackenzie in May 1803. Dodds was a carpenter, but he claimed that he had never had anything to do with the sea and was only doing a job on board the ship on which he was seized. Both Frazier and Captain Mackenzie, however, maintained that Dodds had been to sea in the past and was therefore fair game. The victim came from a Morpeth family which included a number of freemen of that borough. One of the Whig MPs for the town, William Ord, whose seat depended in great measure on support from the freemen but who was not himself *persona grata* with the government, wrote to another local MP, George Burdon, who had good contacts with the Admiralty, to ask him to intervene.[18]

> Dear Mr Burdon,
>
>   I have had an application made to me to endeavour to get a poor man released who has been pressed here; now I know of no means of doing it, but if you should by any way without much trouble to yourself be able to accomplish it I shd. be much obliged to you. His case is that he is a carpenter & never was bred to the sea or has had anything to do with it but was working on board one of Mr Rowe's ships in the Tyne when he was taken & he is the only man that was so taken that has not been released. His Father & Mother are old & infirm & he is the only son they have at home to support them & as they are a family of five in number & all freemen of *Morpeth* I am very anxious if it can be accomplished to get this man released.

Burdon duly passed on this not entirely disinterested plea to the Admiralty, but when Mackenzie repeated his conviction that Dodds had in fact been to sea in the past the Admiralty declined to release the prey.

In addition to operating the routine activities of the Impress Service the Regulating Officer acted as an ordinary recruiting officer. His headquarters—the Rendezvous as it was called—was a reception centre for men joining the navy by a variety of methods other than impressment; there was a trickle of genuine volunteers. Some men joined to obtain a bounty for themselves or their families, while some chose service in the navy as an alternative to prison. A variety of other odd jobs also fell to the Regulating Officer; as a handy administrative official with forces at his disposal he was a useful supplement to local resources, particularly for police functions of various kinds. When in 1809 the Tyne was involved in serious labour troubles sparked off by the high cost of living, and the keelmen again stopped the coal trade, the armed boats of the Impress Service played a part in restoring order, and Captain Charleton was among those officially thanked by Newcastle Corporation.[19] In July 1806 the Regulating Officer was looking after Prussians interned as a result of the Anglo-Prussian tension of that date.[20] In February 1811 at the request of the Home Office the Regulating Officer was told to see to the conveyance of a local man sentenced to transportation to the prison hulks at Greenwich, pending his transfer overseas.[21] A few days later the Admiralty sent down descriptions of some deserters from H.M.S. *Blake* so that the press gangs could keep their eyes open for them.[22]

An unusual case in June 1811 also involved trouble for the Impress Service; four French prisoners escaped from Edinburgh Castle and made their way to Tyneside, where they bribed two local men to take them out to an American ship off the coast. Dissatisfied at the payment received, the two men concerned changed their minds, and all six men were arrested. The men of the Tyne Impress Service played a part in making the arrests, and then the Regulating Officer had to see that the Frenchmen were transferred from their temporary abode in the North Shields House of Correction to the prison ship *Glory* at Chatham; a few months later he had again to see to their return to North Shields as witnesses in the trial of the two local men involved. On this trip they incontinently escaped again, made their way to Alnmouth, and made off out of our story in a pleasure craft ready loaded for a voyage.

All in all, the life of the Regulating Officer was a busy one. In addition to his multifarious activities, he was responsible for the keeping of meticulous records and accounts, which were carefully scrutinized at the Admiralty, and which might be called for at any time if any difficulty arose in any individual case of impressment or expenditure.

Charleton remained Regulating Officer for seven years, until 1810, when he retired from active work and settled down in North Shields as a respected member of local society. He was replaced by Captain Wilson Rathbone, and not long afterwards a renewed shortage of seamen inaugurated another 'hot press'. Rathbone, casting about for expedients to meet this increased demand for men, was struck by the disparity in the arrangements made on the two north-east rivers for the keelmen. The keelmen and the coal interest had assumed that the provision of 80 substitutes had purchased protection for the remainder of the Tyne keelmen for the rest of the war, and Charleton's practice as Regulating Officer had conformed to this interpretation and he had left the keelmen alone. Rathbone now decided to reinterpret the agreement of 1803 and declared that the protection bought then only applied to the keelmen who had actually contributed, so that all who had subsequently entered the trade were now liable to impressment. To point the lesson he pressed a number of keelmen who had since entered the trade, and the Admiralty endorsed his action. Not surprisingly this provoked a great outcry from the coal trade and especially the keelmen, who felt that they had been cheated. At once they downed tools, and again the coal trade of the Tyne was brought to a complete stop.

Another great flurry of activity by the affected vested interests resulted, with Newcastle Corporation and the coal trade trying to induce the navy to abide by the earlier interpretation, without the slightest success, for the Admiralty knew quite well that it held the whip-hand. Rathbone demanded that new levies of substitutes should be exacted from those recently brought into the trade, and the Admiralty returned distinctly cold answers to the complaints of local interested parties. In reply to a detailed protest from the Mayor of Newcastle on 13 April 1811, the Secretary to the Admiralty despatched the following blunt reply:

> I have received and laid before my Lords Commissioners of the Admiralty your letter of the 13th. instant, conveying to me the sentiments of the persons concerned in the coal trade of Newcastle with regard to the impress of certain keelmen employed upon the river Tyne, and referring to an arrangement formerly made with regard to the men in question. In return, I have it in command to acquaint you, for the information of the parties interested in the trade, that, considering the pressing exigency of the service, their Lordships conceive their demands upon the Keelmen to be exceedingly moderate, that they are not disposed to alter the determination which they have come to, and that they have caused directions to be given to the Officer regulating the Impress Service at North Shields, to allow one month for receiving the substitutes, after which, he is to impress such as may be found liable to serve, and for whom substitutes shall not have been provided.

The keelmen had to knuckle under, and to agree to a recurring levy of 10 per cent of substitutes for their new members. With the market for substitutes under heavy pressure in 1811, and the price running at around £60 a man, the keelmen found it impossible to raise in time—even with an extra month's grace conceded—the men needed to meet Rathbone's first demand, and they were therefore forced to ballot among their own numbers to make up the number. After a final dispute as to whether or not keelmen raised in this way could be counted as prime seamen—under pressure from Newcastle the navy conceded this point—the matter was composed in this way. It should be mentioned that the Admiralty was not simply being obstreperous. After all, it was in general clear that all the keelmen were liable to press, and the arrangement now come to was on the same lines as those employed not only for the keelmen of the Wear, but also for other groups elsewhere, such as the Severn watermen and certain groups of Scottish fishermen who were also faced with a quota assessed at a tenth of their adult workers.

This was the last big confrontation between the Impress Service and the local interests. In the last years of the war contacts between local shipping interests and the Impress Service became in some ways closer; in particular there grew up a recognized practice of commutation, whereby pressed men might be released in return for the payment of a cash payment regarded as the price of obtaining a substitute. There had always been a number of cases of a man's release being ordered in return for the provision of a direct substitute or substitutes, but now, unless there was a 'hot press' on, the navy began to accept cash settlements for release in large numbers. For the shipping interest this was a welcome development, and became systematic. A local firm of solicitors, C. and J. Cockerill, closely connected with the shipping interest,[23] became recognized agents for these transactions, and the Admiralty Papers include scores of their letters on this business, showing that the sums involved for release varied in individual cases from £20 to £80 as a rule.

This was one facet of a very clear development in the Impress Service as the war continued; the administration of the system became much more systematic and formalized. One minor example of this can be seen in the certificates of protection issued by Rathbone in 1811 to the keelmen who were then buying their immunity; these documents listed names, ages, heights, complexions, colours of eyes and hair, and any other distinguishing marks of the men concerned, and ended with a formal certificate of protection signed by Rathbone. These forms were typical of a general development in the realm of administrative techniques. The Admiralty itself called for more detailed and more frequent returns from the Regulating Officer of his activity and expenditure. Amongst other forms he had to return regular lists of men raised, stating whether they were impressed, volunteers, recovered deserters or stragglers, or handed over by the civil power, whether they were seamen, landsmen or boys, and exactly what happened to them when they left his hands. He also had to give a precise weekly return of expenditure. Between 26 November 1813 and 31 May 1814 the Tyne Impress Service raised 127 men; of the 117 seamen only 3 were volunteers, 109 were pressed, and 5 were naval stragglers. Only one landsman came from the civil power during these months, while four landsmen and five boys volunteered. At this time the Tyne Impress Service, with its dependent units on the Wear and in the smaller local ports, was costing about £130 per month.

As the war neared its end the Admiralty began to contemplate reductions in the establishment of the Impress Service's establishment. The correspondence of the early summer of 1814 shows an increasing tendency to balance supply of men against cost. There were, however, to be one or two more flurries of activity before the story ended. A sudden temporary shortage of men in April 1814 led to a number of Cockerill's regular requests for commutation being endorsed 'not at present' at the Admiralty, but this was short-lived, and acceptances soon increased again, and definite signs of a running-down of the Service appeared. The specially hired tender was dispensed with, and the Regulating Officer ordered instead to apply to the Flag Officer at Leith whenever he needed transport for his men. The faithful *Eliza* was paid off in June 1814, but her last weeks of service were marked by an ugly incident on 3 May. Among the men detained at the time was Ralph Smith, who had contrived to secrete some tools with him. During a period of almost three weeks he was at work cutting a hole through an iron plate and the foremost bulkhead alongside the press room, replacing every night the piece he had cut, and obscuring the joins by rubbing in rust. Eventually, by the night of 3 May, he had cut a hole right through, measuring 14 by 8½ inches. At 2 a.m. Smith and five other pressed men squeezed through this hole and made their way on deck, four of them through the fore scuttle, the others through the fore hatch. Taking everyone by surprise they overpowered the sentinel, and all six leaped into the Tyne. The tender, however, was deliberately moored well out; one of the six drowned in this attempt and two others, including Smith, were recaptured by boats sent in pursuit. The other three men made their escape.

Rathbone had been replaced as Regulating Officer by Captain J.A. Caulfield when in May 1814 one of the regular reports received the following series of endorsements at the Admiralty:

'Has not this Rendezvous been directed to be broken up?'
'No, Sir.'
'Captain Caulfield to discharge two of the Lieutenants under his orders, retaining those that he likes best, and also the most orderly of the Gangs.'

Some of the other elements in the Impress Service, such as the Gravesend Rendezvous, had already completely closed down, but the Tyne and Wear units continued at a reduced establishment for the time being. Early in July Caulfield was ordered to make further reductions in personnel, and to submit to the Admiralty plans to reduce his monthly expenditure to about £60. Caulfield's scheme proposed a reduction of running costs to about £25 per week; by off-setting half-pay which would otherwise be incurred he calculated that this really meant £18 per week, barely sufficient to keep going two gangs of a midshipman and five men and a midshipman and four men respectively, just enough to man their boats. The Admiralty accepted these estimates.

The large-scale paying-offs which followed victory in 1814 kept the North-East Impress Service in existence into 1815, for the Admiralty found that it still needed its services to provide recruits for the peace-time navy now envisaged. The spring of 1815, with Napoleon's escape from Elba and a renewal of war, brought a renewed flurry of activity, with Caulfield receiving extra officers and men, and things were hectic again till after Waterloo. Then on 5 August Caulfield finally returned to the Admiralty the Press Warrants which had authorized the activities of his unit.

There is a small postscript of interest. In the late summer and autumn of 1815 a major strike of merchant seamen paralysed the ports of Tyne and Wear for two months, and during this struggle the seamen repeatedly turned to the Royal Navy for help. It may have been very natural for them to petition the Admiralty to ask for support in their fight for better pay and conditions, but it is very interesting to note that they turned to Caulfield, the Regulating Officer of the Impress Service, as a suitable local representative for their case, and used him as a channel by which to bring their arguments to the employers and local authorities. Caulfield seems to have discharged this task well, and clearly had some sympathy with the seamen's position. It may be then that the wartime activities of the Impress Service had not been productive of a deep and long-lived bitterness among its victims. This is understandable enough; although there was an increasing volume of complaint against the Impressment system—often because it didn't produce the right kind of recruit in sufficient numbers on demand, as much as for humanitarian reasons—it must be remembered that it was not a kindly age, but one in which hardship was the common lot of the majority of the people. The Impress Service was at the time more usually considered as a necessary evil, and to think back into the early nineteenth century our accepted humanitarian ideas is an exercise of singularly limited utility.

As Professor Michael Lewis has told us in *The Navy in Transition*, Impressment was the contemporary form taken by the established right of the State to conscript the services of its subjects in time of need. It may be worthwhile to take the argument further. The form which this conscription takes will be affected by the extent to which contemporary opinion cares for the welfare of those concerned, and the administrative resources and techniques available. The early nineteenth century was not a period when those possessing power were much concerned to use it to prevent suffering among the lower classes, and the hardship inflicted upon the seamen and their dependants was regarded more lightly in those rougher days than it would be now. Nor were those who suffered normally in a position to exert effective political or social pressure on those in power.

Again, the administrative resources did not exist for the implementation of a system of equable conscription on modern lines; the people had not yet been equipped with personal documentation, nor did the government dispose of the necessary national records or large trained bureaucracy required for such an exercise. Given the need of Britain to maintain a powerful navy, some such system as impressment fitted the circumstances. Yet there is more to be said about the Impress Service and administration. A major factor in the evolution of modern Britain has been the ability of government to devise techniques and obtain resources enabling it to extend the scope of its activities. Although on the one hand the Impress Service exemplifies the limitations of contemporary resources, it yet provides us with a notable early example of administrative development. By the end of the eighteenth century recruitment for the Royal Navy had already ceased to be merely haphazard. Thanks to the work of Barham and his successors at the Admiralty, and the work of the officers of the Service itself, the Impress Service ended its days in 1814-15 as a tolerably sophisticated administrative machine for its day. Then the armed forces were among the greatest manifestations of government activity, and it was in that sphere that administrative techniques were elaborated markedly in these years.[24] It was no accident that serving officers were so often used in the administrative expansions of government in the nineteenth century.

When it is remembered that when Peel went to the Home Office in 1822 its total staff was fourteen clerks, one précis-writer and a librarian, apart from porters and domestic servants,[25] it is by contrast clear how advanced for its day the Impress Service was, with its local agents closely supervised by central authority, its voluminous correspondence and complex records, its own hired and operated shipping, its invention of official forms and elaboration of formal administrative techniques. The year 1815 saw the end of the Impress Service, but it had been a formidable administrative dinosaur, growing to very impressive size before dying as its environment changed. In its own way, remote as it was from the influence of liberal reformers, the Impress Service of the French Wars provides us with one of Professor MacDonagh's 'patterns of government growth', a pattern of government expansion and sophistication carried out by the service itself rather than as the result of expert advice from outside.

After 1815 the press gang ceased to supply the navy with a flow of recruits, but for many years no adequate substitute appeared on the scene.[26] Increasingly, public opinion would not accept the hardships inflicted by impressment, but in the absence of a successful replacement the end of impressment in practice involved great difficulty for the navy. In peace-time for the next half-century and more the Fleet lived a hand-to-mouth existence, barely able to scrape together somehow the men needed to man the shoe-string navy with which Britannia contrived to rule the waves for many years after 1815. The Crimean War saw the difficulties markedly increase, without any very effective solutions yet being propounded. Even in this classical age of British preponderance at sea the end of impressment without its being replaced effectively imposed a serious recruiting problem with worrying effect on efficiency. Fortunately, no crucial need for sending the Fleet to sea in fully mobilized strength emerged before the gap in resources left by the end of impressment had been filled; developments in society, administration and the navy itself made it possible for the Fleet to be reasonably well manned at the outbreak of the First World War by the use of sophisticated administrative techniques impossible a century before.

Reprinted by permission of the Editor, *The Mariners Mirror*

Note

In the quarter of a century since this paper was written, there has been a good deal of research on related topics, and I thought it as well to add a few additional comments to this re-print. There is one factual error to correct, although I have no idea how it occurred. The M.P. described as 'George Burdon' should in fact be Rowland Burdon, M.P. for Durham County, 1790-1806.

I would modify my generalisation about the uncaring nature of British society on either side of 1800. This is partly because of my own subsequent work, which has included study of the expansion of philanthropy, and also because of taking into account other items like the late Professor Michael Flinn's paper on 'The Poor Employment Act of 1817' in *Economic History Review*, 2nd. Series, 14, 1961-2.

While I see no reason to alter the general account of the administrative significance of the Impress Service, I would draw attention to the long tradition of hostility among British seamen to any kind of official registration or listing of them. The French Navy was able to organise such a register long before any British equivalent existed. No doubt the British seamen's distrust of the state could be easily explained.

March 1993   N.Mc.

Notes

1. The principal source used here has been the Admiralty Papers in the Public Record Office, and primarily letters from the Regulating Officers (filed in the Admiralty 1 series) and the Secretary to the Admiralty's out-going letters (filed in Admiralty 2). The disputes about the keelmen are also reflected in a useful collection of relevant documents in the Newcastle city archives. I am grateful to the former Deputy City Archivist, Mr. William Young, for bringing these documents to my attention.
2. It is notable that in Pitt's Quota Act of March 1795 (35 George III, c.9) which imposed levies of manpower on the principal ports, if Newcastle and Sunderland are lumped together (as they were by the Impress Service) they come second only to London.
3. ADM 1/2141, Mackenzie/Admiralty, 25 March 1803.
4. This circumstance may induce us to look more charitably at the conduct of Dillon's superior at Hull at the same time, described by his dissatisfied subordinate as 'content to take his station at the Impress office, and to leave the dirty work to his Lieutenant' *A Narrative of My Professional Adventures, 1790-1839*, by Sir William Dillon, ed. Professor Michael Lewis, II (1956), p.108. Navy Records Society.
5. The last fifty years had seen four attempts, three successful, by pressed men to escape by overpowering the crew of a tender in the Tyne.
6. ADM 1/2141, Mackenzie/Admiralty, 26 March 1803.
7. Three letters from Mackenzie to the Admiralty in these weeks contain harsh criticisms of Frazier.
8. ADM 2/823, Admiralty/Mackenzie, 9 April 1803.

9. ADM 1/1637, Charleton/Admiralty, 23 March 1804. Portland Bill presented a parallel case, which caused even more violent clashes (Lewis, *Social History of Navy*, pp.111-12).
10. Mitchell's affidavit of 3 May enclosed in ADM 1/2141, Mackenzie/Admiralty, 4 May 1803.
11. ADM 1/1644, Charleton/Admiralty, 16 August 1806.
12. An example of an Impress Warrant in vol.III of the Keith Papers, ed. Christopher Lloyd, Navy Records Society, 1955, pp.157 ff. For the keelmen *see* Admiralty affidavit in *Ex Parte Softly*; 1 East 466 in English Reports. This case explicitly upheld the keelmen's liability to impressment. Much information about the earlier history of the keelmen is given in three articles by Dr. J.M. Fewster in *Durham University Journal*, N.S. XIX (1957).
13. ADM 1/2141, Mackenzie/Admiralty, 10 May 1803.
14. Compositions of this kind with local interests were normal in other parts of the country too.
15. The careers of all the officers mentioned in these years have been checked in *The Commissioned Officers of the Royal Navy, 1660-1815*, compiled by the National Maritime Museum and in O'Byrne's *Naval Biographical Dictionary of 1849*. Note also Dillon's view (*op.cit.*, vol.II, p.108) that 'None, generally speaking, but worn-out Lieutenants were employed in that Service'. Some of the Tyne appointees in these years were in poor health.
16. *Ex parte* Edward Boggin; English Reports, 13 East 549.
17. A local informer wrote to the Admiralty, who at once ordered the Regulating Officer to check; he did so the day he received the Admiralty's letter.
18. ADM 1/1633; Charleton/Admiralty, 26 June 1803, 2 July 1803; and enclosures.
19. Mentioned in a group of documents in Newcastle city archives referring to the 1809 troubles.
20. ADM 1/1644, Charleton/Admiralty, 16 July 1806.
21. ADM 2/866, Admiralty/Rathbone, 15 February 1811.
22. There are several other instances in these years of this kind of action. The case of the French prisoners is referred to in a number of letters between Rathbone and the Admiralty in these months.
23. They occur as agents of the shipping interest during the 1815 seamen's strike. See 'The Seamen's Strike of 1815 in North-East England', McCord, N. *Economic History Review*, 2nd. Series, Volume XXI, 1968.
24. An analogy is presented by Pitt's Quota Acts, whose unaccustomed demands sent a noticeable tremor through the creaking machinery of local government—Newcastle Central Library, for example, possesses a copy of a locally printed booklet of 1796. *Forms, with instructions for Filling Them Up, To Be Used in Execution of an Act, Passed the 11th Day of November, 1795, for Raising Men for the Army and Navy, For the Guidance and Instruction of the Constables and Overseers in Northumberland, Newcastle upon Tyne and Berwick*. This handy booklet gives printed copies of forms to be used at all stages of the quota-raising procedure, and accounting procedures for the expense involved.
25. Professor Norman Gash, *Mr Secretary Peel*, p.297 (London: Longmans 1961).
26. Repeated references to manning problems in C.J. Bartlett, *Great Britain and Sea Power, 1815-1853* (Oxford University Press, 1963).

TYNEMOUTH CASTLE & SHIELDS,
from the Bar with Light Ships going into the Harbour

1. Colliers entering the river Tyne, John Dodds, 1797.
Permission of Tyne Wear Museums.

PORT OF *London*

THESE are to certify, whom it doth or may concern, that the bearer *Whyrill Park* is a feaman, aged *Thirty Two* years, is of a *Brown* complexion, *Five feet Ten* inches high, wears *his own light Brown Hair loose & Small Scar on his Thumb. Blue Marks on both Arms Grey Colour Eye* was born at *Scarborough* in the county of *Yorkshire*, and refides at *North Shields* in the county of *Northumberland* that he has been employed *Seven* voyages in the Greenland and Davis's Straits Trade, and is now entered as a *Harpooner* for the ship *Experiment* of *London* whereof *Skelton Vickerman* is mafter, and is to be employed in that ship, in the said Fishery, the next enfuing feafon; and the said *Whyrill Park* hath given fecurity to the fatisfaction of the Honourable Commiffioners of His Majefty's Cuftoms, that he will proceed in the aforefaid ship accordingly.

And by virtue of an Act of Parliament, paffed in the twenty-fixth, and further continued by an Act in the thirty-fecond, thirty-eighth, thirty-ninth, and fortieth years of His prefent Majefty's reign, intituled, "An Act for the further Support and "Encouragement of the Fifheries carried on in the Greenland Seas and Davis's Straits;" the said *Whyrill Park* on producing this Certificate, is not to be impreffed from or out of any coafter or collier, nor from the said ship *Experiment* from the date hereof to the voyage being ended. Given under our hands and feals the *Ninth* Day of *September* One thoufand eight hundred and *one*

Certified by

Mustering Officer.

2. Protection certificate of a Greenland seaman, Whyrill Park, of North Shields, harpooner, 1801. Courtesy of Leonard Park.

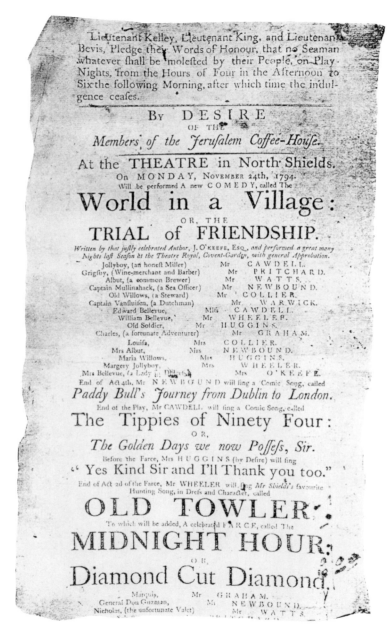

3. Theatre Bill, announcing the suspension of the activities of the press gang at North Shields on 'play nights', 1794.
Courtesy of Literary and Philosophical Society, Newcastle.

4.   A waterfront scene at North Shields, about 1820.
     J W Carmichael.

A SHIP OF THE LINE IN THE DOWNS. VUE D'UN VAISSEAU DE GUERRE DANS LES DUNES.

5. Ships of the Line in the Downs.
Up to half of the crew of a large man of war were likely to have been impressed.

ALL Gentlemen Seamen and able bodied Landmen that are willing to enter on board his Majesty's Ship SYREN, Edmund Dod, Esq; Commander, a fine new Frigate of 24 guns, (launched at Howden Dock, and to be sheathed with copper; from the fine construction of her bottom, is supposed will be as fast a sailing vessel as any in the Navy.) Let them repair to Capt. Dod, at his Lodgings in Newcastle, or on board the Syren in the river, or to Lieut. Adamson, in Newcastle; Lieut. Okes, at Shields; Lieut. Campbell, at Sunderland; or Lieut. Mennell, at Blythe; where they shall meet with every encouragement.

His Majesty's Bounty of FIVE POUNDS will be given to every able Seaman, TWO POUNDS TEN SHILLINGS for every ordinary Seaman, and THIRTY SHILLINGS for every able bodied **Landman,** that will enter to serve on board the said Ship.   GOD *save the* KING.

FERRET, and the WEASEL,

Carrying each 25 Men, and well provided with Carronades, 12 Pounders, &c. commanded by Captains HENRY CLENNEL ROMER, and JOHN BROWN. These Vessels are most remarkable fast sailors, and drawing little water, are admirably calculated to hunt out a lurking Enemy.

Let all able and true-hearted North Country Men, who are desirous of making their fortunes, and wish to distinguish themselves by a spirited attempt to serve their country; and whose hearts glow with an honest indignation against the unnaturally united Enemies of Great Britain, now quickly step forward and apply at the Rendezvous, the Sign of the Peacock, on the Keyside, where they shall receive such encouragement as the gallant Tars of Old England can desire.

6.   Advertisement placed in the Newcastle newspapers by Edmund Dod, calling on volunteers to serve in the *Syren*.
Advertisement announcing the fitting out of two privateers the *Ferret* and *Weasel* for a cruise against the Dutch.

RICHES and HONOUR!

Now's the Time to make your Fortune, my Boys! and drub the Dutch.

Dutch Guilders, Double Louis d'Ors, and Spanish Dollars,

TO all Gentlemen Sailors, able Landsmen, Sea-boys, and others, that incline to make their fortunes; they now have an opportunity of doing it, by entering on board that well known remarkable fast sailing cutter, lately the Cromartie Castle, now called the

DREADNOUGHT,

of 16 four and six-pounders, 10 swivel guns, and 60 men, the brave Capt. WILSON POTTS, Commander, (late of the Scarborough man of war) now laying at New-castle, where she is (with all expedition) fitting out for a *Three Months* Cruize against the Dutch and other Enemies of Great Britain.

Any person wanting to try their fortune, will meet with good encouragement by applying to Captain Wilson Potts, on board the said vessel; Mr Jonathan Wharton, the Bird in Hand, North Shields; Mrs Wheatley, the Turk's Head, South Blyth; Capt. George Adams, on the Quay, Newcastle; Mr Thomas Morris, the Anchor and Hope, Ewes-Burn-bridge; or at Mr Henderson's, the White Lion, Sunderland.

BOUNTY MONEY.

For every able Seaman, Six Guineas; for every ordinary Seaman, Four Guineas; for every able Landsman, Three Guineas; for every Sea-boy, Two Guineas and a Half; for every Land boy, One Guinea.

N.B. Every able Seaman who enters before Saturday the 24th inst. shall receive One Guinea extra of the Bounty, every Landsman Half a Guinea, every good Sea-boy a Crown, and every good Land-boy Half a Crown.

Any Persons who have served in the Militia will meet with good encouragement.

God save the King, and Down with the Dutch.

To be SOLD to the highest Bidder [...] At the house of Mr Ralph Lewens, in Holy Island, on Thursday the 22d instant, between the hours of twelve and one in the afternoon.

7.   Advertisement calling for volunteers to serve on board the *Dreadnought*, privateer, 1781.

8.   Greenland whalers like the *Cove* were often commissioned with "letters of marque" because they were heavily manned and well armed. The *Cove* received a "letter of marque" during the American War of 1812.
Courtesy of Palmer Collection.

THE ORIGINS AND REGULATION OF EIGHTEENTH-CENTURY BRITISH PRIVATEERING

by David J. Starkey

The term 'privateering' embraced a variety of activities common in the maritime wars of the eighteenth century. Principally it related to the privately-owned vessels licensed by the state and set out with the specific intention of seizing enemy property on the high seas. In Britain these private men-of-war ranged in size and ambition from the tiny 'cockleshells' of the Channel Islands which harassed French coastal traffic in the adjacent waters, to the ocean-going squadrons fitted out in London and Bristol to cruise more distantly in search of Spanish register ships and French East Indiamen. Also within the 'privateering' compass lay the armed merchantmen, vessels primarily concerned with trade but equipped with commissions to take advantage of a chance meeting with a potential prize. Indeed, some enterprises combined predatory and commercial aims, a private man-of-war perhaps abandoning a barren cruise to take in a cargo, or an armed trader indulging in commerce-raiding on the return leg of a voyage. Such varied activities shared much common ground, of course: their main purpose was to earn profits for the individuals concerned in the venture; their means were often violent, involving the forced appropriation of foreign ships and property; and their legitimacy was undoubted, these acts of private maritime warfare being formally sanctioned by the state.

While their aims and means had close affinities with those of pirates, privateers were also closely related to state navies since their authority was valid only in wartime and against enemy property. Thus, privateers inevitably carried the taint of piracy despite their potential utility to the state in an age when destruction of enemy commerce was afforded a high strategic priority. This paper examines the peculiar, slightly paradoxical, status of privateering in eighteenth-century warfare by focusing on the evolution of the phenomenon and on the regulatory measures adopted by the state to maximise its efficiency as a tool of war. Such an examination is intended to throw some light on the nature of British privateering enterprise in the wars of the eighteenth century.[1]

Origins

Although the phrase 'private man-of-war' was not coined until 1646 and the term 'privateer' dates back only to 1664,[2] it is clear that forms of privateering had been practised much earlier. The activity, in fact, developed from a number of sources which can be traced back to medieval times. Certainly its roots lie in the ancient custom of reprisal. This was a means by which an individual could redress, by force if necessary, a proven grievance against a foreign subject. It was a measure of last resort for the wronged party could only petition his sovereign for 'letters of marque, and reprisal' once all efforts to obtain satisfaction using the legal processes of the foreign state had failed. Once granted, the 'letters of reprisal' empowered the petitioner to recover the amount of his loss from any of his transgressor's compatriots, with any surplus accountable to his own sovereign. Such a device made possible minor acts of war without breaking the general peace but it was open to abuse as it led to the proliferation of counter reprisals. Nevertheless, reprisals were sought and granted throughout the Middle Ages; in England, the procedure was regulated by statute in the early fifteenth century, while in France requests for grants of reprisal were judged in Parlement.[3]

From this concept of the redress of individual loss by reprisal in peacetime there evolved the notion of 'general' reprisals against an enemy nation in wartime. Nations could justify acts of war as retaliatory measures against an aggressor, and therefore reprisals against the subjects of the offending nation were permissible. In July 1739, for instance, general reprisals were granted against Spanish commerce in retaliation for the depredations purportedly committed by the Spanish *guarda-costas* in the Caribbean, while in December 1780 the reluctance of the United Provinces to respond to a series of published British grievances provoked the authorisation of general reprisals against Dutch trade and shipping. Moreover, the terminology of medieval reprisals survived and was still applied to the 'general' reprisals of the later era. Thus, the terms 'letter of marque',[4] 'letters of marque and reprisal' and 'letters of reprisal' were used to describe the licences granted to privateers from the mid-sixteenth century, though this usage was inappropriate in the strictest sense, as the rights implied by such grants were only applicable in peacetime.[5]

Another origin of privateering is to be found in the use of private ships by the state for purposes of war in the days when royal navies were non-existent or inadequate. In England, the Norman kings depended upon the coast towns, particularly the Cinque Ports, to mobilise a set number of ships during an emergency, occasionally, as in 1242, ordering all the vessels of the Channel ports to commit every possible injury upon the enemy at sea.[6] In the fourteenth and fifteenth centuries there were several instances of 'putting out to contract the keeping of the seas',[7] while Henry VIII made use of a large number of hired merchant ships to augment his fledgling navy in the French wars of the 1540s. It was therefore customary for the state to hire or impress privately-owned vessels, authorising them, by virtue of 'commissions', to act as ships of war. Though the growth of navies in the seventeenth century meant that the state became less reliant on the merchant service, the capacity to commission merchant vessels was retained and on occasion it was invoked to authorise acts of private maritime warfare. For example, in the American Revolutionary War, when it was theoretically impossible to grant reprisals against the rebellious North

American colonists, who were still subjects of His Britannic Majesty, commissions were issued to authorise the seizure of goods carried in contravention of the 1775 Prohibition of Trade Act.[8]

If the letter of marque and the privateer commission derived from separate origins, the difference in the application of their respective powers was purely technical by the eighteenth century. Indeed, it was the Admiralty's practice to address 'the commanders of such merchant ships and vessels as may have letters of marque, or commissions, for private men-of-war'.[9] This terminological elasticity was stretched still further by the application of the term 'letter of marque' to a particular form of eighteenth-century privateering vessel, the armed merchantman, as well as to the document she carried. This strain of 'privateering' derived from a third origin of the activity, and again it can be traced back over the centuries. Trading vessels had long since carried arms to protect themselves against assailants, particularly in the more distant trades to Africa, the West Indies and Asia. In such dangerous areas they might be called upon to use their weapons and a successful action against a pirate or enemy ship might result in its capture. However, it became a principle of maritime law that a captor without a commission had no legal title to his prize, which was usually condemned as a 'droit and perquisite' of the Admiralty. Therefore, to reap the rewards of such an encounter, or to profit from a meeting with a weak or incapacitated enemy vessel, owners of these armed traders began to take out commissions for their vessels in wartime. Thus, by the eighteenth century, the privateering forces of belligerent powers included a number of merchant vessels, armed primarily to deter aggressors, but licensed to take prizes should the opportunity afford itself in the course of a commercial voyage.

In broad terms, two separate types of privateering activity had developed from these origins by 1700. In the first place, the commissioned merchantman, or 'letter of marque' as she became known, clearly evolved from the customary need to arm vessels engaged in long-distance trades. The 'letter of marque' carried a cargo, and its safe delivery was the captain's main priority. To this end he might delay his departure until the sailing of a convoy or he might seek the company of a British man-of-war or privateer in potentially dangerous waters, he might gamble and sail independently taking care to avoid areas where enemy men-of-war or *corsaires* were known to cruise.[10] Either way, captains of commissioned trading vessels were usually under orders to make prize of enemy property if the opportunity arose. Such a capture might add greatly to the profit of a commercial venture and the captain and his crew would also benefit from the distribution of prize money on top of their basic wages. Amongst the commissioned merchantmen were the vessels owned or hired by the great chartered companies. The Royal Africa Company, the Hudson's Bay Company and, most significantly, the East India Company, all took out letters of marque for their vessels during wartime. As with other armed traders, the licences carried by these ships added a predatory dimension to their regular trading voyages.

The second type of privateer, the private man-of-war, was a descendant of the private reprisal vessels and the merchant fighting ships of the medieval and early modern age. These were the privateers proper—the additional forces that formed 'an effective constituent of England's naval power'.[11] Some were purpose-built, though the majority were merchantmen converted for the task of commerce destruction. Naval vessels were occasionally bought and fitted out as private men-of-war; in February 1745, for instance, a group of Bristol merchants purchased H.M.S. *Hastings* and adapted her for privateering.[12] Prize vessels were sometimes redeployed as privateers with some, such as the *Dover's Prize* of London and *Kitty's Amelia* of Liverpool, having their names altered to bear testimony to their origin. Private men-of-war embarked on cruises rather than voyages, carrying little, if any, cargo. Generally, they were heavily armed and naval terminology was applied to the officers and crew; thus, privateers carried lieutenants rather than mates, midshipmen instead of apprentices and the crew often included a surgeon and a gunner.[13] Indeed, the size and composition of its crew were probably the most distinctive features of the eighteenth-century private man-of-war. Invariably this predator would be heavily manned in relation to her size. Large crews were necessary to man the extra guns normally carried by the private man-of-war and, most significantly, to provide prize crews to navigate captured vessels to a friendly port. A successful cruise might involve the seizure of a number of prizes and large crews were necessary to secure prizes and allow the private man-of-war to remain at sea.

A further distinctive feature of a private man-of-war's crew was that, unlike its counterpart in the merchant service or the Royal Navy, it received no regular wages. An advance, or bounty, was usually paid to the men as they enlisted,[14] but any further remuneration normally depended upon the seizure and condemnation of a prize. The articles of agreement drawn up before the commencement of each cruise laid down the division of any spoils. In Britain the proceeds of a cruise were generally divided into two parts with the owners of the vessel receiving one half, the other going to the crew.[15] The latter portion would then be divided amongst the crew according to the number of shares allocated to each man. In the case of the *Southwell* of Bristol, the crew's half was divided into 262½ shares, with the commander owning 12 shares, the first lieutenant, master and doctor holding 6 shares each, the 'able sailers' holding a single share apiece and the 'ordinary sailers' allotted three-quarters of a share each. Thus, when the *Southwell*'s fifth cruise produced net receipts of £251 7s 3d, each of the twelve owners received £11 16s 3d and Commander John Engledue pocketed £5 15s 0d, each share being worth 9s 7d.[16]

Regulatory Devices

While the armed merchantman and the private man-of-war embarked with different intentions, both types of privateer were subject to an identical system of regulation. This system had evolved over time, its greatest development occurring in the seventeenth century as the rapid growth of overseas trade and state navies obliged the maritime powers to formalise their relations. Within the code of international maritime law which developed to meet this need, the control of privateering—and its definition as a legitimate activity, distinct from piracy—assumed a principal position. In Britain, privateering activity was regulated by the High Court of Admiralty, a body responsible for the issue of letters of marque and privateer commissions and the condemnation of prizes. To obtain a licence, the intending privateer commander—or someone acting on his behalf—was required to attend the Admiralty Court, in Doctors' Commons, London,[17] and produce a 'warrant from the Lord High Admiral of England and Ireland for the granting of a letter of marque or commission'. Then he was obliged to make a declaration before the Admiralty judge consisting of a 'particular true and exact account of the ship or vessel' to be commissioned.[18] Furthermore, a bail or surety had to be provided by reputable guarantors of the good behaviour of the commander and his crew.

These two devices—the commander's declaration and the guarantor's bond—were the principal means by which the Admiralty Court controlled the issue of letters of marque. The declaration, first introduced in 1689, detailed the characteristics of the vessel and named the officers and principal owners, clearly identifying the ship and those responsible for her actions. The taking of sureties was the method traditionally employed by the authorities to ensure that privateers acted in accordance with the Admiralty's 'instructions to privateers', drafted at the commencement of hostilities. If the instructions were contravened the bond was liable to prosecution in the Admiralty Court. Its amount, fixed by the Anglo-Dutch Marine Treaty of 1674, varied with crew size; if more than 150 men were on board the bail was £3,000, and if less, it was £1500.[19] Under the terms of the 1708 Cruisers and Convoys Act the Court was obliged to grant a letter of marque to any commander making a declaration and providing bail. However, complaints from neutrals about the excesses of British privateers forced the government to pass the Privateers' Act of 1759,[20] which imposed some restrictions on the issue of commissions. This legislation gave the Admiralty the discretion to refuse licences to privateers under 100 tons burden carrying fewer than 12 guns of 4lbs weight of shot and 40 men, although their issue remained obligatory for larger ships.[21] Furthermore, it tightened up the regulations on sureties, forbidding the commanders and owners to stand bail for themselves, obliging the guarantors to swear that they were worth the sum in which they were bound, and instructing the marshal of the Court to enquire into their circumstances.

The declaration having been made and the bail provided, the commander was granted a letter of marque authorising him to attack enemy property. Before leaving port, however, the commissioned vessel had to be examined by the local Customs Collector who issued a certificate as to the size, manning and armaments of the ship. If the privateer embarked without this clearance pass or if the force of the ship was less than that stated in the letter of marque, the latter was null and void and the commander liable to imprisonment. Once at sea the conduct of the cruise was bounded by the 'instructions to privateers' issued to each recipient of a letter of marque. In addition, privateer owners often provided their commanders with copies of relevant treaties and books to guide their behaviour. Thus, John Engledue of the *Southwell* privateer was presented with a 'Book of maritime affairs and Copy of the Marine Treaty between us and the Dutch',[22] while Richard Fitzherbert of the *Dreadnought* was given a copy of 'Naval Trade and Commerce' and instructed to comply with its provisions, particularly with regard to the 1674 Anglo-Dutch treaty.[23]

These various instructions embodied a code of conduct within which the commander and crew were supposed to operate. The code was modified over time, but five main areas of control were evident.[24] Firstly, the rights of neutrals were to be respected, hence the concern of owners that the 1674 Marine Treaty should be observed. The spoliation of neutrals, particularly the Dutch, sometimes embarrassed the British government which made sporadic attempts to limit the privateering attack to contraband goods.[25] The second aim of the instructions was to prevent cruelty to the crews of captured vessels; thus, Francis Ingram, managing owner of the *Enterprize* of Liverpool, implored her commander, James Haslam, to refrain from plundering any prisoners of their clothes and bedding and to treat them 'with all tenderness and humanity, consistent with your own safety'.[26]

Thirdly, the instructions were designed to eradicate any suppression or distortion of evidence. Captors were required, therefore, to bring three or four members of the prize vessel's crew into port for examination as to the nature of the voyage and the capture. Papers, sea briefs, bills of lading and any other documents found on board the prize were to be brought into port intact and without interference to help determine the legality of the capture. The fourth area of regulation forbade the embezzlement of cargoes and the sale of goods before condemnation. The fifth concern of the instructions was to ensure that prizes should be brought to trial. Thus, captors were obliged to convey their prizes to a British, colonial or friendly port where examination of the prize, witnesses and evidence could take place. The practice of ransoming vessels at sea was gradually restricted, and finally outlawed in the American Revolutionary War,[27] thereby ensuring that prizes could be properly adjudicated.

Penalties were fixed for those who transgressed the instructions, although how rigorously they were enforced is open to some doubt, particularly in the colonies.[28]

However, the instructions constituted a set of rules for the proper conduct of the privateer at sea. If a vessel was arrested by the commissioned vessel and there were sufficient grounds for its prosecution it was to be dispatched to a home or friendly port with at least three of its crew as witnesses, its bulk unbroken and any documentary evidence intact.[29] When a prize was landed, its arrival was to be reported to the customs officials of the port and subsequently a libel was exhibited against it in the Admiralty Court.

Members of the prize vessel's crew, preferably the captain and two officers, were then subjected to a preparatory examination as to the legality of the capture. This examination was normally conducted in the port of landing, often at an inn, before the local magistrate and public notary. Witnesses were obliged to answer a set of standing interrogatories, some twenty or so questions intended to discover the nationality of the prize, its crew and owners, the origin and destination of its cargo, and the nature and location of its seizure. On the completion of the preparatory examinations a monition was set up in a public place, usually outside the Royal Exchange in London, ordering all persons interested in the prize vessel or cargo to stake their claim within twenty days. If nobody claimed within the stipulated time the judge of the Admiralty Court was to take into consideration the preparatory examinations, together with any evidence taken from the prize, and pronounce sentence.

This procedure was straightforward and swift in cases where the prize was uncontested, but in other cases, when interested parties made a claim to the property in question, the system was more complex. If the evidence of distant witnesses was required, the judge ordered an appraisement of the disputed vessel or goods to be made before awarding them to the claimant, by interlocutory decree. On receipt of the property the claimant was required to give security to restore the appraised value should the sentence go against him. Either party could appeal against the decision to a superior court, the Court of Prize Appeals, which could delay the final pronouncement for months or even years.

Thus, from the issue of his letter of marque to the condemnation of his prizes a variety of devices, amounting to a system of control, restrained the activities of the British privateersman. The competence of this system is difficult to judge. However, it is clear that its application not only involved a number of agencies, but also required a substantial contribution from the privateersman himself.

Policing the Privateersman

The regulatory framework within which British privateers operated was well established by the eighteenth century. Its chief function, as far as the state was concerned, was to maximise the military utility of private ships-of-war by restricting their predatory designs to the trade and shipping of enemy nations. The extent to which the authorities could control privateers depended upon two main factors, the efficiency of the legal and administrative system erected to deal with general reprisals, and the effectiveness of the means deployed to police private warships on the high seas. In essence, this entailed the smooth operation of the prize division of the High Court of Admiralty, and, at sea, the vigilance and impartiality of the Navy, together with a degree of self-discipline on the part of the privateersman.

Evidence relating to these matters is somewhat fragmentary, largely because those who successfully transgressed the rules of the predatory game were naturally reluctant to chronicle their misdemeanours. However, there is sufficient information to suggest that the system of control and the methods of policing private men-of-war were sufficient to curb the worst excesses of privateersmen and to ensure that commerce-raiding only rarely jeopardised Britain's relations with neutrals and allies. The High Court of Admiralty, for instance, seems to have discharged its prize duties with some competence. This was a somewhat quixotic tribunal, a bastion of the civil law in which the interests of litigants were represented by proctors who presented the depositions of witnesses, exhibits and other forms of evidence to a judge presiding and adjudicating without a jury.[30] It was an institution which experienced its share of administrative problems; for instance, in 1778, it was reported that the...

> warrants granted to privateers for making reprisals on the French were, either through negligence, inattention or design, sealed with a wrong seal; the consequence thereof is that they must be resealed, which will protract their sailing for seven or eight days at least.[31]

Moreover, as the Admiralty Court was the only place in which prize law could be dispensed, the proctors were in a monopoly position, a factor reflected in the heavy fees charged for their services.[32] Political pressure could also influence the Court's decisions. For instance, in 1758-9, with the neutral United Provinces threatening to declare war, a number of privateersmen were sentenced to death for plundering Dutch ships, while a series of contentious cases were settled in favour of Dutch claimants in the Prize Appeals Court, verdicts which owed more to diplomatic considerations than to natural justice.[33]

Yet for all its idiosyncrasies and occasional lapses, the High Court of Admiralty dealt effectively with a large volume of prize business during wartime. This is clearly apparent in the vast extent and remarkable internal consistency of the archive which survives. Hundreds of thousands of documents relating to countless predators and captures are preserved and logically arranged in the HCA collection. In these holdings, the expertise of the Court's servants in negotiating the complexities of prize law, the technicalities of life at sea and the conflicting interpretations of international treaties is readily apparent.[34] Furthermore, this specialist tribunal regularly invoked its power to punish British privateersmen who exceeded their authority. The papers of the Prize Appeals Court abound with the successful claims of wronged neutral or allied citizens, with costs and damages generally awarded against the errant captor.[35]

That such impartiality had a wider impact is suggested by the orders given to Captain Patrick Galloway by his employers. Thus, he was to desist from bringing in neutral ships,

> as it will never answer our ends, & on the contrary would make us odious to all traders here [London], & at the Court of Admiralty, & put us to great charges and damages.[36]

Of course, the High Court of Admiralty could only act upon the cases brought before it and the evidence submitted by litigants. The extent to which privateersmen plundered vessels, mistreated prisoners, distorted evidence or otherwise ignored their instructions is uncertain. However, it is clear that there were means of detecting, and of deterring, such misdemeanours. The Navy was the principal detective agency. There were occasions when the discipline of errant privateersmen formed a specific part of a naval captain's duty. For instance, in 1760, 'the commanders of all the King's ships' were ordered to locate the infamous privateersman John Patrick and 'to take him out of his ship wherever they meet with him'.[37] Generally, however, it was on an incidental basis that men-of-warsmen were called upon to administer discipline to privateersmen. A chance encounter at sea, for instance, revealed to Lord Hervey, captain of H.M.S. *Daphne*, that James Vercoe, commander of the *Fox* privateer of Plymouth, had plundered a neutral merchantman, while the officers of H.M.S. *Berwick* discovered stolen and smuggled goods aboard the *Dreadnought* privateer of Newcastle during a similar meeting.[38]

This policing role was just one facet of the complex relationship which existed between public and private naval forces in the eighteenth century. In theory, private men-of-war supplemented the state navy in the attack upon enemy trade and the defence of home shipping. There were innumerable occasions when privateers performed such a supportive role, though their contributions were usually small in scale and of an incidental nature.[39] But it was competition rather than co-operation that generally characterised the relations between naval and privateering personnel. Thus, as service in both forms of warship was rewarded by a share in any properties taken, there was invariably a degree of rivalry in the pursuit of prizes. Disputes over the division of spoils between privateersmen and men-of-warsmen frequently occupied the time of the Prize and Prize Appeals Courts, particularly during those phases when the commerce-raiding war was at its height.[40]

The search for seamen was a further source of friction. Private men-of-war were labour-intensive vessels and attracted large numbers of men at times when naval requirements meant that demand far exceeded supply in the seafaring labour market.[41] Though privateersmen were normally protected from impressment, complaints from privateer owners indicate that such immunities were often ignored.[42] Here, the Navy's recruitment drive might harmonise conveniently with its policing function, for as well as delivering miscreants to the proper authorities, naval officers sometimes took a more direct form of disciplinary action by pressing guilty men into naval service. Such immediate retribution was visited upon 29 privateersmen who mutinied aboard the *Princess Augusta* of Bristol, on the thieves and smugglers discovered in the *Dreadnought* of Newcastle, on the angry members of the *Winchelsea*'s crew in their violent efforts to obtain compensation from the vessel's owners, and no doubt on countless other troublesome seafarers.[43] To the privateersman, therefore, the naval officer might appear as both press-master and policeman, an authoritarian duality which perhaps explains the bitterness evident in the 'New Song on the *Blandford* Privateer':[44]

Why should we here our time delay, in London void of pleasure,
Let's haste away to Biscay Bay and ransack there for treasure,
Here we must weep and play bo-peep to shun the damn'd press-masters,
We live in strife, even die in life, confin'd by catch-pole bastards.

While irregularities in the privateersman's behaviour at sea might be detected and summarily punished, deterrence was probably a much more effective means of control. This is not to suggest that offenders faced extraordinarily harsh physical punishments if apprehended. Rather, the chief deterrent—and probably the single most important facet of the regulatory system—at work aboard a British private man-of-war was the self-discipline that the economic rationale of the commerce-raiding business instilled into her crew. In general, privateersmen earned no wages, their sole remuneration arising out of the proceeds of any prizes taken and subsequently condemned. Each seafarer was therefore a shareholder in the profits of the venture. Accordingly, it was in the interests of all concerned, men as well as owners, to maximise the prize fund to be divided at the conclusion of the enterprise. While this vested interest served to discourage plunder and embezzlement, it positively encouraged the commanders and crew of commissioned vessels to follow their instructions, for behaviourial and procedural irregularities might precipitate a rash of claims in the Admiralty Court, thereby protracting the legal proceedings and adding to the costs of the venture. Such threats to the earnings of privateersmen, many of whom viewed their transitory occupation as a once-in-a-lifetime opportunity to secure a fortune, were instrumental in ensuring that the great majority of ventures did not stray beyond the regulatory limits laid down by the state. Quite simply, observing the guidelines enhanced the chances of securing the extraordinary profits which commerce-raiding promised. While this may not always have been the case in earlier times, by the eighteenth century British privateering enterprise, that ancient, tense amalgam of private interest and public service, had developed a regulatory logic of its own.

University of Exeter

Notes

1. The issues discussed in this paper are treated at length in David J. Starkey, *British Privateering Enterprise in the Eighteenth Century*, (Exeter University Press, 1990).
2. John W. Damer Powell, *Bristol Privateers and Ships of War*, (Bristol: Arrowsmith, 1930) p.xvi.
3. For a detailed analysis of the theory and practice of reprisals in medieval Europe, see Maurice H. Keen, *The Laws of War in the Late Middle Ages* (Routledge & Kegan Paul, 1965), pp.218-38.
4. This was sometimes 'mark', 'mart' or 'march'. Although its etymological source is unclear it seems likely that the word 'marque' derived from "march"—from the marcher's right to avenge his wrongs by armed force. Keen, *Laws of War*, p.231.
5. Francis R. Stark, *The Abolition of Privateering and the Declaration of Paris* (New York: Columbia University Press, 1897) pp.51-5.
6. Stark, *Abolition of Privateering*, pp.50-1.
7. Reginald G. Marsden, *Law and Custom of the Sea* (Navy Records Society, 1915), I, pp.115-8.
8. Privateer commissions against the colonists were authorised by 17 George III, c.7. 'An Act for Enabling the Commissioners...to Grant Commissions'... .
9. Public Record Office (PRO), High Court of Admiralty (HCA), 26/4. 'Instructions to Privateers', 29 March 1744.
10. Such ships were known as 'runners'.
11. John K. Laughton, *Studies in Naval History* (Longmans, 1887) p.201.
12. Powell, *Bristol Privateers*, p.137.
13. Walter E. Minchinton, 'Piracy and Privateering in the Atlantic, 1702-76' in *Course et Piraterie* (Paris: Commission Internationale d'Histoire Maritime, 1975), I, p.300.
14. For instance, a total of £518 3s 6d was advanced to the crew of the *Southwell* before her fifth cruise in May 1746. The officers received 5 guineas each, 3 guineas went to the 'able sailers', with two guineas advanced to every 'ordinary sailer'; Avon County Library (ACL), Papers of the *Southwell* privateer, 24651.
15. There were regional variations, however. See Starkey, *British Privateering Enterprise*, pp.73-8.
16. ACL, Papers of the *Southwell* privateer, 24651.
17. In the colonies, the vice-admiralty courts granted commissions and condemned prizes, though abuse of the system appears to have been common. See Richard Pares, *Colonial Blockade and Neutral Rights, 1739-1763* (Philadelphia: Porcupine Press, 1975) pp.53-64.
18. Quoted from 'Instructions to Privateers', PRO, HCA 26/60.
19. The declarations made in the Admiralty Court between 1689 and 1815 are to be found in PRO, HCA 26/1-104; the respective bail documents are included in the HCA 25 classification.
20. 32 George II, c.25. The preamble states that 'whereas repeated complaints have of late been made by divers outrageous Acts of piracy and robbery, committed on board great numbers of ships, more particularly by the crews of small ships, vessels or boats being, or pretending to be, English privateers'... .
21. The alleged depredations were blamed on the smaller privateers, especially those operating in the Channel.
22. ACL, Papers of the *Southwell* privateer, 24651.
23. ACL, Papers of the *Southwell* privateer, 24651.

24. For a detailed discussion of the privateers' instructions, see Pares, *Colonial Blockade*, pp.53-64.
25. The definition of contraband varied over time and from country to country and was always a source of diplomatic tension between Britain and neutral powers. See Stark, *Abolition of Privateering*, pp.68-98; Pares, *Colonial Blockade*, pp.92-4.
26. Liverpool Record Office (LRO), Account books of the *Enterprize*, 387 MD 45.
27. See Pares, *Colonial Blockade*, pp.19-26. Ransoms were finally prohibited by the 1778 Prize Act, 19 George II, c.67.
28. The many irregularities of colonial privateers and prize courts are discussed by Pares, *Colonial Blockade*, pp.109-32.
29. Commanders were generally directed by their employers to escort valuable prizes to port to reduce the risk of recapture by an enemy man-of-war or privateer, or re-possession by the prize vessel's crew. Prize crews usually navigated less valuable prizes to the nearest home port, leaving the privateer to pursue its cruise.
30. See F.J. Wiswall jr, *The Development of Admiralty Jurisdiction and Practice since 1800*, (Cambridge University Press, 1970).
31. *Morning Chronicle and London Advertiser*, 19 August 1778.
32. See Starkey, *British Privateering Enterprise*, pp.308-15.
33. *Gentleman's Magazine*, 29 (1759), 496, 604.
34. See John C. Appleby and David J. Starkey, 'The Records of the High Court of Admiralty as a Source for Maritime Historians' in David J. Starkey, ed., *Sources for a New Maritime History of Devon*, (Exeter: Devon County Council, 1986), 70-86.
35. See PRO, HCA 42 & 45.
36. PRO, C 108/318. Creagh & Fallet to Patrick Galloway, 2-3 March 1703.
37. Damer Powell, *Bristol Privateers*, pp.207-13.
38. PRO, HCA 45/12; *Newcastle Chronicle*, 9 June 1781.
39. See David J. Starkey, 'The Economic and Military Significance of British Privateering 1702-1783' *Journal of Transport History*, 9 (1988), 50-9.
40. See David J. Starkey, 'British Privateering against the Dutch in the American Revolutionary War, 1780-1783' in Stephen Fisher, ed., *Studies in British Privateering, Trading Enterprise and Seamen's Welfare, 1775-1900*, (Exeter University Press, 1987) 1-17.
41. See David J. Starkey, 'War and the Market for Seafarers in Britain, 1736-1742' in L.R. Fischer and H.W. Nordvik, eds., *Shipping and Trade 1750-1950: Essays in International Maritime Economic History*, (Pontefract: Lofthouse, 1990) 25-42.
42. For instance, see Francis Ingram's complaints in LRO, Account Books of the *Enterprize*, 387 MD 45.
43. Damer Powell, *Bristol Privateers*, p.157; *Newcastle Chronicle*, 9 June 1781; PRO, C 103/130. Richard Taunton to Thomas Hall, 26 August 1746.
44. Damer Powell, *Bristol Privateers*, pp.140-1.

MAKE YOUR FORTUNE MY BOYS!
AND DRUB THE DUTCH

PRIVATEERING AND THE NORTH EAST COAST
IN THE LATER EIGHTEENTH CENTURY

by Tony Barrow

By the middle of the eighteenth century the principal ports of North East England had become important centres of business and commerce. The growth of the coal trade and the expansion of the Baltic and north European trades in particular, stimulated the development of the local economy and came to dominate the employment of shipping in the region. By the end of the century Whitby, Sunderland and Newcastle were numbered amongst the leading outports in the kingdom, in terms of their shipping tonnage, and each had become an important centre of shipbuilding and maritime related industry. The subsidiary ports of the region like Stockton-on-Tees, Blyth and Berwick-upon-Tweed exhibited a similar picture of growth and prosperity. It is equally true, however, that this picture of growth was often distorted by the effects of the frequent wars of the eighteenth century. Merchants and shipowners were especially vulnerable to the economic warfare that targeted their ships, impounded their cargoes and captured their seamen. But at the same time the outbreak of hostilities presented shipowners with new opportunities for the employment of their vessels. Some chose to continue their ships in trade and were able to use higher wartime freight rates to offset increased insurance and wage costs. Alternatively, the owners of many of the larger ships at Whitby and Shields engaged them in government service as hired transports. Perhaps the most spectacular option was to employ their vessels as privateers.

> 'We call privateering'...wrote one contemporary observer...'the expeditions of private individuals during war, who, being provided with a special permission from one of the belligerent powers, fit out at their own expense, one or more vessels with the principle of attacking the enemy'...[1]

The earliest references to privateering from the North East coast occur during the later middle ages, but the first detailed account of it comes from the early seventeenth century. In 1626 John Butler, a Newcastle merchant and a member of the Company of Hostmen, complained to the Privy Council and sought redress for the capture and subsequent ransoming of his ship, the *Robert*, by a Dunkirk privateer. Butler received 'Letters of Marque' licencing him to fit out the *Revenge* which duly sailed from the river Tyne on a 'cruize'. Butler's *Revenge* was, perhaps, the North East's first modern privateer. No doubt other local ships were employed as privateers during the Dutch Wars and the Spanish War of Succession. But it was during the wars of the second half of the eighteenth century that privateering enterprise from local ports reached its peak.

Privateering activity manifested itself in two main ways. Some private ships of war were equipped for the sole purpose of attacking enemy shipping on the high seas. Others were armed merchantmen, primarily concerned with trade, but provided by the High Court of Admiralty with letters of marque which entitled them to capture enemy vessels or those belonging to neutral powers suspected of carrying cargoes intended for enemy use.

During the Seven Years War (1756-1763) the shipowners of Newcastle and Sunderland licenced ten vessels with letters of marque and a single ship, the *Barnard*, sailed from Stockton-on-Tees. All of these vessels were armed merchantmen principally engaged in distant foreign trades. They were also amongst the largest ships at their respective ports. Table 1 summarises the detail of each of these vessels. The *Dolphin* of Newcastle was a Greenland whaler, one of a small fleet of whaleships

Table 1

Letters of Marque issued to vessels at North East Ports during the Seven Years' War (1756-1763)						
Date of commission	Tons	Guns	Men	Victualling period (months)	Name	Port
13.08.1756	500	9	20	3	Blackett	Newcastle
21.03.1758	300	12	50	6	Dolphin	Newcastle
17.06.1757	200	8	25	6	Gottenburg Merchant	Newcastle
09.12.1758	310	14	30	6	King of Prussia	Newcastle
27.08.1757	350	18	40	12	Loyalty	Newcastle
13.03.1759	320	12	25	8	Loyalty	Newcastle
08.12.1756	300	16	40	6	Nancy	Newcastle
24.11.1756	400	10	20	3	Swan	South Shields
05.07.1756	400	9	20	2	Betty's Increase	Sunderland
14.07.1757	230	16	36	3	Britannia	Sunderland
18.03.1757	400	10	40	6	Duke William	Sunderland
01.11.1756	250	16	35	6	Barnard	Stockton

Source: PRO, HCA 25/40 and HCA 26/5-12.
I am grateful to Dr. David J. Starkey, University of Exeter, for the basic information provided in Tables 1-4.

which began sailing from the river Tyne in this period. Whaling ships were well armed and heavily manned and usually had no difficulty in qualifying for a letter of marque at little extra expense to the owners. In announcing the departure of the Tyne whalers in 1757 the *Newcastle Journal* boasted that...

'as they are completely fitted with great guns and small arms, manned with stout seamen, and are to act in concert with Mr. Brown[2] as commodore...if any French privateer should have the assurance to attack them, 'tis presumed he will meet with a warm reception'...[3]

Table 2

	**Letters of Marque issued to armed merchant ships at North East ports during the American Revolutionary War (1777-1782)**
Enemy	Date of commission	Tons	Guns	Men	Victual-ling period (months)	Name	Port
FR	21.01.1780	450	9	16	3	Delight	N. Shields
DU	10.01.1781	150	8	16	3	Dublin	N. Shields
FR	27.02.1779	450	12	21	2	English Hero	N. Shields
FR	14.06.1779	500	10	18	4	Good Agreement	N. Shields
DU	03.09.1782	400	12	18	6	Happy Return	N. Shields
DU	30.12.1780	300	12	18	6	Present Succession	N. Shields
FR	27.02.1779	470	24	60	9	Prince William	N. Shields
US	27.02.1779	476	24	60	9	Prince William	N. Shields
SP	07.07.1779	470	24	60	9	Prince William	N. Shields
FR	11.11.1778	360	14	20	4	Burdon	S. Shields
SP	03.09.1782	400	12	18	6	Happy Return	S. Shields
FR	03.06.1779	350	30	65	12	Neptune	S. Shields
US	03.06.1779	350	22	65	12	Neptune	S. Shields
SP	13.07.1779	350	30	65	9	Neptune	S. Shields
US	23.10.1778	260	30	30	12	Peggy	S. Shields
FR	23.10.1778	250	30	30	12	Peggy	S. Shields
FR	02.02.1781	240	10	15	3	Blessing	Sunderland
FR	27.05.1779	240	12	12	2	Jane	Sunderland
DU	10.01.1781	220	7	20	3	Nimrod	Sunderland
US	08.12.1778	300	20	40	12	Preston	Stockton
US	08.12.1778	350	20	40	12	Amphitrite	Stockton

continued...

Table 2 (cont'd)

Enemy	Date of commission	Tons	Guns	Men	Victual-ling period (months)	Name	Port
US	04.09.1778	250	-	-	-	Florida	Newcastle
FR	04.09.1778	250	-	-	-	Florida	Newcastle
DU	12.01.1781	250	10	20	3	Garnet	Newcastle
FR	23.10.1778	240	28	30	9	George and Jane	Newcastle
US	23.10.1778	240	28	30	9	George and Jane	Newcastle
FR	07.09.1778	300	14	20	2	Hardwicke	Newcastle
FR	27.10.1778	450	12	21	3	John	Newcastle
US/FR	16.02.1779	400	14	50	6	John and Margaret	Newcastle
DU	30.12.1780	400	18	50	6	John and Margaret	Newcastle
FR	04.05.1779	400	11	20	3	Johns Adventure	Newcastle
FR/DU	23.01.1781	180	16	20	6	Kitty	Newcastle
US/FR	19.11.1778	378	28	60	9	Lady Georgina	Newcastle
US/FR	23.01.1779	400	12	18	2	Mary	Newcastle
FR	14.04.1779	300	12	20	6	Mary	Newcastle
FR	04.03.1779	400	8	16	2	Minerva	Newcastle
DU	30.12.1780	260	18	50	6	Minerva	Newcastle
FR	25.02.1779	500	16	18	3	Montague	Newcastle
US	13.08.1777	340	10	44	8	Priscilla	Newcastle
FR	16.09.1778	340	10	44	6	Priscilla	Newcastle
DU	30.12.1780	348	10	44	6	Priscilla	Newcastle
FR	04.03.1779	400	8	16	2	Richard	Newcastle
FR	27.10.1778	500	12	21	3	Shafto	Newcastle
FR	07.06.1779	300	14	18	6	Tynemouth Castle	Newcastle

Source: PRO HCA 26/33-70
NB: Letters of marque were issued separately against each of the hostile powers.

Although the whalers were well equipped to defend themselves, laden colliers were slow, lightly armed and vulnerable to the attacks of enemy warships and privateers. In May 1757 three French privateers chased a fleet of 51 colliers into Whitby harbour, and in 1757-58 the *Maréchal de Belleisle*, a French frigate of 44 guns, was reported to have captured over 70 prizes, most of them in the North Sea.[4] Occasionally a combination of courage and good seamanship, or just good luck, enabled the odd vessel to escape. In 1757 the *Ann* of Shields, carrying five guns and eight men, engaged a French privateer of 14 guns and 150 men for over four hours. The Frenchman was forced to break off the engagement and the *Ann* struggled back into the river Tyne.[5]

The level of interest in privateering from the ports of North East England during the Seven Years' War was about the same as during the War of Austrian Succession (1739-1748), but it was insignificant compared to the national total. Between 1756 and 1763, 2,676 vessels sailed from British ports with letters of marque and they accounted for 382 prizes.[6] None of the privateers fitted out in the Tyne or the Wear appear to have shared in this success, although several prizes captured by other ships were sent into Shields. However, this picture altered substantially during the American War of Independence when privateering activity from Great Britain reached its apogee.

The American colonists began to take action against British shipping in August 1776, but Lord North's administration was at first reluctant to retaliate in the hope that the colonists could be reconciled. By April 1777 however, this proved to be a forlorn hope and the British government sanctioned the issue of letters of marque. Subsequently the entry of France, Spain and the Netherlands on the American side, between July 1778 and December 1780, stimulated the further growth of privateering enterprise. For the first time, the merchants and shipowners of North East England showed an interest in fitting out privateers of the predatory type, as well as the armed merchantmen which had characterised local involvement in privateering during the Seven Years War. There were, in total, 43 vessels licenced as privateers at North East ports between 1777 and 1782, almost four times as many as there were in the previous conflict. These ranged from small 40-ton former customs cutters like the *Elizabeth* of Berwick and the *Ferret* and *Weasel* of Newcastle, to the 500-tonners *Good Agreement* of North Shields and *Montague* of Newcastle. Table 2 summarises the letters of marque issued to armed merchantmen owned in North East ports between 1777 and 1782.

The first letter of marque was issued to the owners of the *Priscilla*, a Greenland whaler, on 13 August 1777 after her return from the whaling grounds. It was usual in this period for Greenland ships like the *Priscilla* to be re-employed in the coal trade during the autumn and winter months. The presence of a well-armed ship with a letter of marque amongst the collier fleet proved to be a useful deterrent. The *Priscilla* confronted and fought off two French privateers which had attacked colliers near Aldeburgh on the Suffolk coast during the autumn of 1780.[7] The *Priscilla* and another whaler the *John and Margaret* also received letters of marque for their voyages to the Davis Straits in 1781. This made sound economic sense since Dutch whalers were the principal competitors for British vessels engaged in the Greenland trade. With letters of marque British whalers might legally take advantage of an opportunity to capture a Dutch Greenlandman complete with its cargo of blubber and bone. The value of sailing with a letter of marque was amply demonstrated by a number of Greenland ships during the American War.[8] In March 1782 two large London whalers, the *Achilles* and the *Marianne*, in company with two English privateers, the *Swallow* and the *Eagle*, captured the *Valck*, a Dutch privateer and carried her into North Shields. The *Valck*, together with all of her equipment, was sold at North Shields in August 1782. In addition, on 29 November 1783, £185 in head money was paid to the crews of the four English vessels, indicating that there had been 37 men on board the *Valck* at the time of her capture.[9] Successes of this kind were generally the preserve of private ships of war which deliberately hunted the vessels of belligerent states. Newcastle merchants equipped their fair share of this type of privateer during the American War and each of the vessels fitted out at Berwick were commerce raiders as well. Details relating to these letters of marque are contained in Table 3.

Table 3

Letters of Marque issued to private ships of war at North East ports during the American Revolutionary War (1778-1782)							
Enemy	Date of commission	Tons	Guns	Men	Victual-ling period (months)	Name	Port
FR/US	10.11.1778	250	36	120	6	Antigallican	Newcastle
SP	02.07.1779	250	36	120	6	Antigallican	Newcastle
FR/SP/US	25.02.1780	250	36	120	4	Antigallican	Newcastle
DU	26.12.1780	250	36	120	6	Antigallican	Newcastle
FR/DU/US	16.02.1781	80	22	60	3	Dreadnought	Newcastle
DU	19.01.1781	107	20	30	6	Eagle	Newcastle
FR/DU/US/SP	21.04.1781	40	7	20	6	Ferret	Newcastle
US/SP	23.12.1778	300	30	100	6	Heart of Oak	Newcastle
FR	02.07.1779	300	20	100	6	Heart of Oak	Newcastle
FR/DU/US/SP	21.04.1781	40	7	20	6	Weasel	Newcastle
FR/DU/SP	28.12.1780	50	8	25	3	Alarm	Tynemouth
FR/DU/US/SP	26.01.1781	40	16	40	3	Elizabeth	Berwick
FR/DU/US/SP	26.03.1781	160	18	110	6	Intrepid	Berwick
FR/DU/US/SP	19.11.1781	110	10	25	6	Tartar	Berwick

Source: HCA 26/33-70.
 ` NB: Letters of marque were issued separately against each hostile power.

The best known and, as it turned out, the most successful, were the *Antigallican* and the *Heart of Oak* of 36 and 30 guns respectively. At 250 and 300 tons both ships exceeded the average tonnage of privateers fitted out at east coast ports during the American War of Independence.[10] In common with the ownership patterns at other ports, the owners of the *Antigallican* and the *Heart of Oak* were described simply as 'merchants', a general term which covered a range of interests. Emerson Headlam, a principal owner of the *Heart of Oak*, was a noted Gateshead shipbuilder. Joseph Lamb, Robert Lisle and John Coulson, principal owners of the *Antigallican*, were general merchants with interests in the Baltic, Coal and Greenland trades. Lisle and Coulson had owning interests in the *Priscilla* as well. The letter of marque for the *Dreadnought*, which fitted out in 1781, described her principal owners, George Adams, Thomas Barker and Henry Scott as...'Esquires of Newcastle'...[11]

The *Heart of Oak* and the *Antigallican* sailed from the river Tyne in March 1779 and preyed on French, Dutch, Spanish and American shipping in the Western Approaches, Bay of Biscay and Straits of Gibraltar. The first prize to the *Heart of Oak* was a French privateer carried into Dover in May 1779. It was a small vessel and had little value...'the public are probably more benefitted from this little success than the proprietors'...[12] The *Heart of Oak* went on to capture four more prizes, including Spanish and Swedish merchantmen trading between Marseilles and Cadiz, and an American brig, the *Success*, taken off the Azores in August 1779 laden with best Madeira wine for the colonies. The Swedish vessel, *Le Duc Charles de Sudemaine*, was carried into Lisbon where she remained for almost two years before her neutral status was finally established.[13] Her cargo of pipe staves was sold for the benefit of the owners but much of the profit gained is likely to have been swallowed up by litigation costs.

The capture of the *Comte d'Estaing*...'50 leagues to the west of Lisbon'...in February 1780 seemed to represent the most valuable prize to be captured by the *Heart of Oak*. The *Newcastle Courant* was certainly optimistic and initially estimated the vessel and her cargo to be worth £20,000...

> 'The *Heart of Oak*, privateer of this port with her prize the *Comte d'Estaing* are safe arrived at her moorings in the river Thames. She proves to be an outward bound East Indiaman laden with bale goods, wine etc. and is likely to be a very valuable prize'...[14]

The prize papers tell a rather different story. The *Comte d'Estaing* was certainly a French East Indiaman bound from Lorient to Mauritius with stores for the French garrison there. But she proved to be a British built ship, formerly called the *Neptune* of Whitehaven, which had been captured in the Atlantic in 1778. The valuable cargo was confiscated and sold for the benefit of the investors but the ship was restored to her original owners at Whitehaven and Captain Plowman of the *Heart of Oak* received £335 salvage.[15] Perhaps it was the disappointment of the transaction which induced the owners of the *Heart of Oak* to advertise her for sale soon afterwards.

Make Your Fortune my Boys! And Drub the Dutch

59

In the long run the *Antigallican* was probably a more successful privateer than the *Heart of Oak*. She was certainly active for a longer period of time. Ironically, her first 'cruize' almost ended in disaster and she is not reported to have captured any prizes before October 1779. In June 1779 the *Antigallican* had narrowly escaped a brush with the French fleet off Cape Finistere...'but having excellent heels cleared their chase'...[16] In October the *Antigallican* captured the *Vrow Susannah*, a Dutch merchant ship bound from Barcelona to Ferrol, and soon afterwards it was reported that...

'The *Antigallican*, privateer of Newcastle, Captain Kinghorn, has taken the *Havanneiro* a Spanish ship from Havannah to Cadiz laden with hides, sugar, coffee, logwood and hard dollars. She is valued at £200,000.'[17]

Three further prizes fell to the *Antigallican* between February 1780 and June 1781, before her career as a privateer came to an end.[18]

At the same time as British privateers were acting against enemy shipping, French, Dutch and American privateers frequently appeared off the North East coast. The trade of the smaller ports of the region was especially vulnerable to this privateering activity...

'the only thing now wished for or wanted is a brisker coal trade'...wrote Lord Delaval's agent at Seaton Sluice...'Privateers so much invest the coast that the collier vessels do all incline to go in fleets and not otherwise which practice greatly hurts the trade of this port'...[19]

Further to the north Berwick smacks and small coasting sloops employed in the corn trade were also affected. In February 1783...

'a large lugsail privateer with 3 masts, supposed to be Dutch,...[has] been hovering on and off the Bamburghshire coast and pursued some vessels...she drove on shore near Embleton a corn vessel from Alnmouth to Leith...and set her on fire'.[20]

In August 1779 the redoubtable American privateer, John Paul Jones, appeared several times off Tynemouth Castle and the Yorkshire coast causing consternation in the coal trade. In September, near Flamborough Head, he fell in with the Baltic fleet and fought the famous engagement with the *Serapis*. Dozens of colliers fell victim to the attacks of these enemy privateers during the American War; there was also the usual crop of adventures. The escape of the *Jenny* in July 1780[21] and the desperate struggle of the *Alexander and Margaret* are amongst the most well known. The collier brig *Alexander and Margaret* of North Shields was attacked by 'the notorious English pirate' Daniel Fall, commander of the 18 gun cutter privateer *Fearnought* of Dunkirk. The captain of the *Alexander and Margaret*, David Bartleman, resisted the attack for over two hours but, with the mate dead and himself dangerously wounded, Bartleman was forced to strike his colours and ransom the ship for 400 guineas. The second mate, David Michael, was taken as a hostage until the ransom was paid.

Bartleman managed to navigate the *Alexander and Margaret* into Yarmouth where he died of his wounds a fortnight later.[22]

David Bartleman lost his life during a period of renewed interest in privateering investment on both sides of the North Sea. The outbreak of hostilities with the Netherlands led to a 'mania' of investment in small privateering vessels. In Britain, letters of marque against Dutch shipping became available on 26 December 1780, and over 200 were issued by noon of that day, including one for the *Antigallican* of Newcastle.[23] Two days later, on 28 December, the *Alarm* of Tynemouth also received a letter of marque. In February-March 1781 the Newcastle newspapers carried a number of advertisements calling for volunteers to serve on board privateers then fitting out in the river Tyne. The imminent departure of the *Dreadnought* carried the boldest headlines...

'Nows the time to make your fortune my Boys! and drub the Dutch'...[24]

Dreadnought eventually sailed from Shields on 7 March 1781. She was followed in May by...'two excellent nimble cutters'...the *Ferret* and the *Weasel*.[25] None of these small privateers appear to have had much success. The *Dreadnought* carried two merchant ships, the *Helena* and the *Gretentia*, into the river Tyne soon after her departure, but they proved to be Danish ships and were released to continue their voyages.[26] The *Dreadnought* was sold at Leith in July 1781 and was returned to general trade. The small privateers fitted out at Berwick were much more successful.

In February 1781 the *Elizabeth* captured at least two prizes, including the *Hay Fortune*, from Emden to Harlingen, which she carried into Harwich.[27] The other Berwick privateers, *Intrepid* and *Tartar*, both captured American vessels, the former in particularly dangerous circumstances...

'The vessel was taken amongst the rocks near the Naze of Norway and was chased there by the *Intrepid* [which]...in working for shelter from a storm was driven on the rocks, and being aground was fired at and many shot took effect in the sails and sides of the said *Intrepid* privateer—on suspicion that she was an American vessel this deponent (William Renwick, the master of the *Intrepid*) sent his boat on board and took possession of her as a prize...[but]...before the boats crew could get on board the whole crew deserted...and got on shore...[and] fired several musket shot at the privateers crew'.[28]

The *Intrepid*'s prize and her cargo of tobacco, sugar, beaver skins and logwood was subsequently sold at Berwick in October 1781.[29] It was William Renwick, this time as the master of the *Tartar*, who was responsible for the capture of another American ship in 1782. Its cargo of...'best Muscovado sugar'..., rum, tobacco, cotton and coffee was sold at Berwick in September 1782.[30] The valuable cargo of this unidentified American ship may well have been the last to be auctioned for the benefit of privateering investors anywhere on the North East coast before the American war ended.

Make Your Fortune my Boys! And Drub the Dutch

61

Table 4

Letters of Marque issued to vessels at North East Ports during the French Revolutionary War 1793-1801						
Date of commission	**Tons**	**Guns**	**Men**	**Victualling period (months)**	**Name**	**Port**
08.09.1795	486	12	40	12	Brunswick	Newcastle
10.11.1795	486	12	40	12	Brunswick	Newcastle
27.04.1801	403	8	32	6	Canada	Newcastle
27.04.1801	403	8	32	6	Canada	Newcastle
05.03.1799	397	10	45	6	John and Margaret	Newcastle
06.09.1793	220	10	16	6	John and Elizabeth	Newcastle
26.02.1793	112	8	30	1	Mermaid	Newcastle
22.10.1795	112	10	30	2	Mermaid	Newcastle
01.12.1796	112	10	30	2	Mermaid	Newcastle
27.04.1801	407	8	32	6	Minorca	Newcastle
27.04.1801	322	2	24	4	Nice	Newcastle
16.02.1796	481	10	40	12	Ocean	Newcastle
30.07.1798	481	12	40	6	Ocean	Newcastle
24.08.1801	395	10	36	12	Hercules	S. Shields
12.10.1799	401	10	30	6	Ajax	Sunderland
10.04.1800	925	20	50	6	Lord Duncan	Sunderland

Source: PRO, HCA 26/73-75 and 81-87.

The decade which separated the end of the American war from the outbreak of the French Revolutionary War was one of rapid growth in the shipping industry. The restoration of normal trading relations and the release of ships and seamen from government service, enabled merchants and shipowners to concentrate their energies on developing new commercial opportunities. In addition to the steady growth of the coal and coasting trades, and the expansion of trade with Europe, a number of local merchants sought to develop their interests in the Atlantic trades as well. By the outbreak of the French Wars in 1793 there were well over 1,000 ships registered at North East ports between the Tees and the Tweed. With such a significant shipping base it is surprising that the return of wartime conditions did not stimulate a renewed interest in privateering enterprise. Although a substantial number of locally owned merchant ships were certainly entered into the transport service, relatively few ships were employed as privateers. There were 11 vessels commissioned with letters of marque at North East ports between 1793 and 1801, and their details are summarised in Table 4. With the exception of the *Mermaid*, a former customs cutter, all of them were armed merchant ships primarily concerned with trade. They included the 925-ton *Lord Duncan* of Sunderland, the largest vessel to be commissioned as a privateer anywhere on the North East coast between 1756 and 1801, and the *John and Margaret*, a Davis Straits whaler. This large Greenland ship was owned by Thomas and Francis Hurry, shipbuilders of Howdonpans, and had sailed with letters of marque during the American War [see Table 2]. It is not known if the *John and Margaret* or any of the other local ships commissioned with letters of marque met with success.

Most of the references to privateering activity off the North East coast between 1793 and 1801 relate to the activities of British warships against French and Dutch privateers and the loss or capture of local vessels. Greenland whalers were amongst the earliest victims of the trade war. The veteran *Priscilla* which had figured so prominently during the American Revolutionary War, was captured by a French frigate during a voyage from Archangel to London in 1794. Another whaler, the *Sunderland* was taken off Shetland in 1795. But it was the attrition rate amongst the collier fleets which gave the most cause for concern throughout the 1790s, despite the exaggerated claims of a report in the *Newcastle Courant*...

> 'a double chain of cruizers is now stationed from the Firth of Forth to the Nore by which the coasting trade in the North receives the most perfect protection!'[31]

In reality ships engaged in the coasting trade were usually obliged to look to their own defence and Berwick smacks acquired a considerable reputation in this respect. Berwick smacks were usually armed with six or eight, eighteen pounder guns, small arms and boarding equipment, and could normally outsail even the swiftest privateers. Although they were not immune to capture themselves, a contemporary observation that...'small privateers do not effect to come alongside of a Berwick smack'...[32] was clearly not an idle boast!

There were a number of occasions when these well-known coasting ships became involved in offensive as well as defensive actions against enemy privateers. In 1796 the *Kelso*, belonging to the Union Company, rescued the sloop *Tay* of Arbroath from a French cutter privateer in a short engagement off Cromer.[33] There were similar engagements involving Berwick smacks in 1804, 1806 and 1808, the latter a particularly sharp fight off Newbiggin Point.[34] The collier brigs of Blyth and Seaton Sluice were more vulnerable to these predatory attacks which often occurred close inshore. In March 1801 Lord Delaval's agent at Seaton Sluice wrote...

'the *Honoured*, one of two ships that sailed out of our roads at 8 o'clock last night was captured by a French lugger privateer off the Bates (St. Mary's Island) about two miles distant soon after 10 o'clock, two hours or a little more after she had weighed anchor'...[35]

The capture of this Seaton Sluice collier, though perhaps not typical, was nevertheless a familiar experience for many shipowners in the age of the privateer.

Notes

1. *An Essay on Privateers, Captures and Recaptures*, de Martens, M. London, (1801).
2. Captain William Brown, master of the *Swallow* of Newcastle. Brown later commanded Greenland whalers at London, notably the *Marianne* which captured two prizes in 1781 and 1782.
3. *Newcastle Journal*, 16 April 1757.
4. *The Arctic Whalers*, Lubbock, B. Brown Son and Ferguson, Glasgow, (1937). p.97.
5. 'The Maister', *A Century of Tyneside Life*, Haswell, G.H., Walter Scott Ltd., London (1895). p.40.
6. 'The Economic and Military Significance of British Privateering 1702-83', Starkey, David J. in *Journal of Transport History*, 9 (1988).
7. *Newcastle Courant*, 21 October 1780.
8. In 1781 the *Marlborough* of Whitby and the *Caroline* of Hull both indulged in some commerce raiding before they sailed to the Whale Fishery. The *Caroline* captured a Dutch merchant ship ...'supposed to be worth £5000'... In April 1781 the Liverpool whaler *Betsy* with a letter of marque, was reported to have taken another Dutch vessel the *Johannes* ...'from St. Eustatia to Amsterdam with 292 hogsheads of sugar, 100 hogsheads of tobacco, 158 bags of coffee, 103 bags of cocoa and 9 casks of indigo'... *Newcastle Courant*, 21 April 1781.
9. PRO, ADM 43/29. Bounty money was payable to the crew of private ships of war at the rate of £5 per head of crew on board the captured vessel at the commencement of the engagement. I am grateful to Dr. David J. Starkey for this information.
10. The average tonnage of all privateers fitted out at ports between Berwick and the river Thames was 179 tons. *See* Minchinton, W.E. and Starkey, D.J. 'Characteristics of Privateers operating from the British Isles against America, 1777-1783', Table 3, p.260 in *Ships, Seafaring and Society, Essays in Maritime History*, Runyan, T.J. (Ed.). Wayne State University Press, (1987).
11. PRO, HCA 26/42.
12. *Newcastle Courant*, 15 May 1779.
13. PRO, HCA 32/312.
14. *Newcastle Courant*, 11 March and 18 March 1780.
15. PRO, HCA 32/297/5.
16. *Newcastle Courant*, 17 July 1779.
17. *British Privateering Enterprise in the Eighteenth Century*, Starkey, D.J. University of Exeter Press, Exeter (1990), p.230.

18. These were: the *Ligeria*, a Spanish privateer carried into Lisbon on 4 November 1780—*see* PRO, HCA 32/390/1; the *St. Olaf*, a Swedish merchant ship carried into Falmouth in February 1781—*see* PRO, HCA 32/416/10; and the *Le Bienvenu*, a French privateer which was sold at North Shields on 13 August 1781—*see* PRO, HCA 32/282/12 and *Newcastle Courant*, 2 June 1781.

19. John Crooks to Sir John Hussey Delaval, 30 May 1779. Northumberland Record Office, 2/DE4/4/13.

20. *Newcastle Courant*, 15 February 1783.

21. In January 1781 at the annual general meeting of a ship insurance association at the Three Indian Kings Tavern, the crew of the *Jenny* were presented with cash rewards for beating off the attentions of two French privateers which had attacked them in the North Sea in July 1780. The master received 'a valuable gold watch', the mate and the carpenter 5 shillings each, the seamen 4 shillings and the apprentices 2 shillings. *Newcastle Courant*, 13 January 1781.

22. Haswell, *op.cit.* p.41.

23. 'British Privateering against the Dutch in the American Revolutionary War, 1780-83'. Starkey, D.J. in *Studies in Privateering, Trading Enterprise and Seamen's Welfare*, Fisher, S. (Ed.) Exeter University Press (1987). p.7.

24. *Newcastle Chronicle*, 9 February 1781.

25. *Newcastle Courant*, 24 March 1781.

26. *Newcastle Courant*, 31 March 1781.

27. *Newcastle Chronicle*, 10 March 1781.

28. PRO, HCA 32/469/48.

29. *Newcastle Courant*, 29 September 1781.

30. *Newcastle Courant*, 24 August 1782.

31. *Newcastle Courant*, 13 August 1796.

32. Goode's Directory of Berwick-upon-Tweed, Part I, 1806.

33. *Newcastle Courant*, 12 March 1796.

34. *Newcastle Advertiser*, 5 March 1808.

35. William Bryers to Sir John Hussey Delaval, 28 March 1801.

ALSO AVAILABLE from BEWICK PRESS

R Challinor and B Ripley, *The Miners' Association: a Trade Union in the Age of the Chartists*, UK £8.95

Owen R Ashton, W E Adams: *Chartist, Radical and Journalist (1832–1906)*, UK £8.95

Archie Potts, Jack Casey: *The Sunderland Assassin*, UK £6.95

Nigel Todd, *The Militant Democracy: Joseph Cowen and Victorian Radicalism*, UK £8.95

Brenda Whitelock, *Timepieces of Newcastle*, UK £8.95

Archie Potts, *The Wearside Champions*, UK £8.95

Stan Shipley, *Bombardier Billy Wells*: *the life and times of a boxing hero,* UK £9.95

Bewick Press,
132 Claremont Road
Whitley Bay
Tyne & Wear,
NE26 3TX